ARABIC ART
IN COLOR

Edited by
PRISSE D'AVENNES

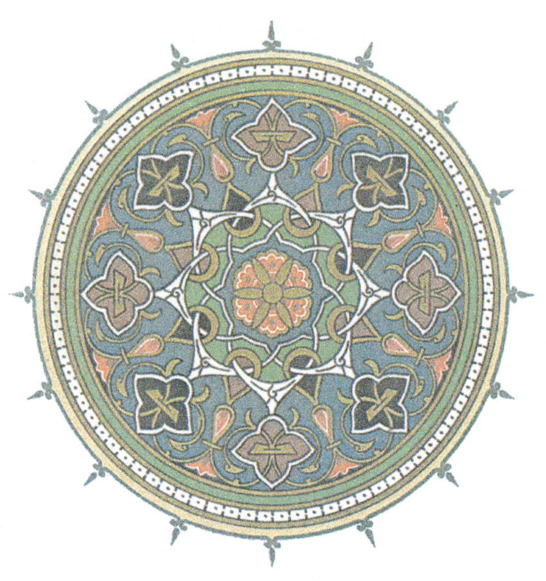

DOVER PUBLICATIONS, INC.
MINEOLA, NEW YORK

PUBLISHER'S NOTE

From 1869 through 1877 the French art historian Prisse d'Avennes published *L'art arabe,* a sumptuous set of plates illustrating a wide range of art treasures located in and around the city of Cairo (along with a few comparison pieces from European collections). Ever since the Arab conquest of Egypt in the seventh century, Cairo has been one of the great centers of Islam. In its mosques and palaces, Prisse d' Avennes discovered rare architectural ornament, tiles, wood carvings, paintings on walls and ceilings, woven hangings, carpets, paper appliques and illuminated books. These and a variety of other riches had either been made locally or had poured into Cairo through the centuries from as far away as Persia in the east and Moorish Spain in the west. From the sixteenth century onward, Turkish influence is very strong. Prisse d'Avenne's exquisite plates were the first publication of most of this hitherto neglected and unknown material.

From these rare folio volumes we have selected fifty lithographic plates containing 141 designs and motifs that constitute a grammar of Islamic decorative art. In his introduction to *L'art arabe,* Prisse d'Avennes explicitly stated that one of his principal goals was to furnish exciting visual ideas to the decorative artists of his own day. It is in the same spirit that we now publish this representative selection from that monumental publication.

Bibliographical Note

Arabic Art in Color is a new selection of plates from: Prisse d'Avennes, *L'art arabe d'après les monuments du Kaire depuis le VIIe siècle jusqu'à la fin du XVIIIe* (text volume and three plate folios), Paris, Ve. A. Morel et Cie, 1877; and *La décoration arabe... extraits du grand ouvrage "L'art arabe" de Prisse d'Avesnes* [sic]..., Paris, J. Savoy & Cie, 1885. The Publisher's Note and the English-language captions were prepared specially for the present edition.

DOVER *Pictorial Archive* SERIES

International Standard Book Number
ISBN-13: 978-0-486-23658-2
ISBN-10: 0-486-23658-7

Manufactured in the United States by LSC Communications
23658714   2018
www.doverpublications.com

Oval ceramic wall panel.

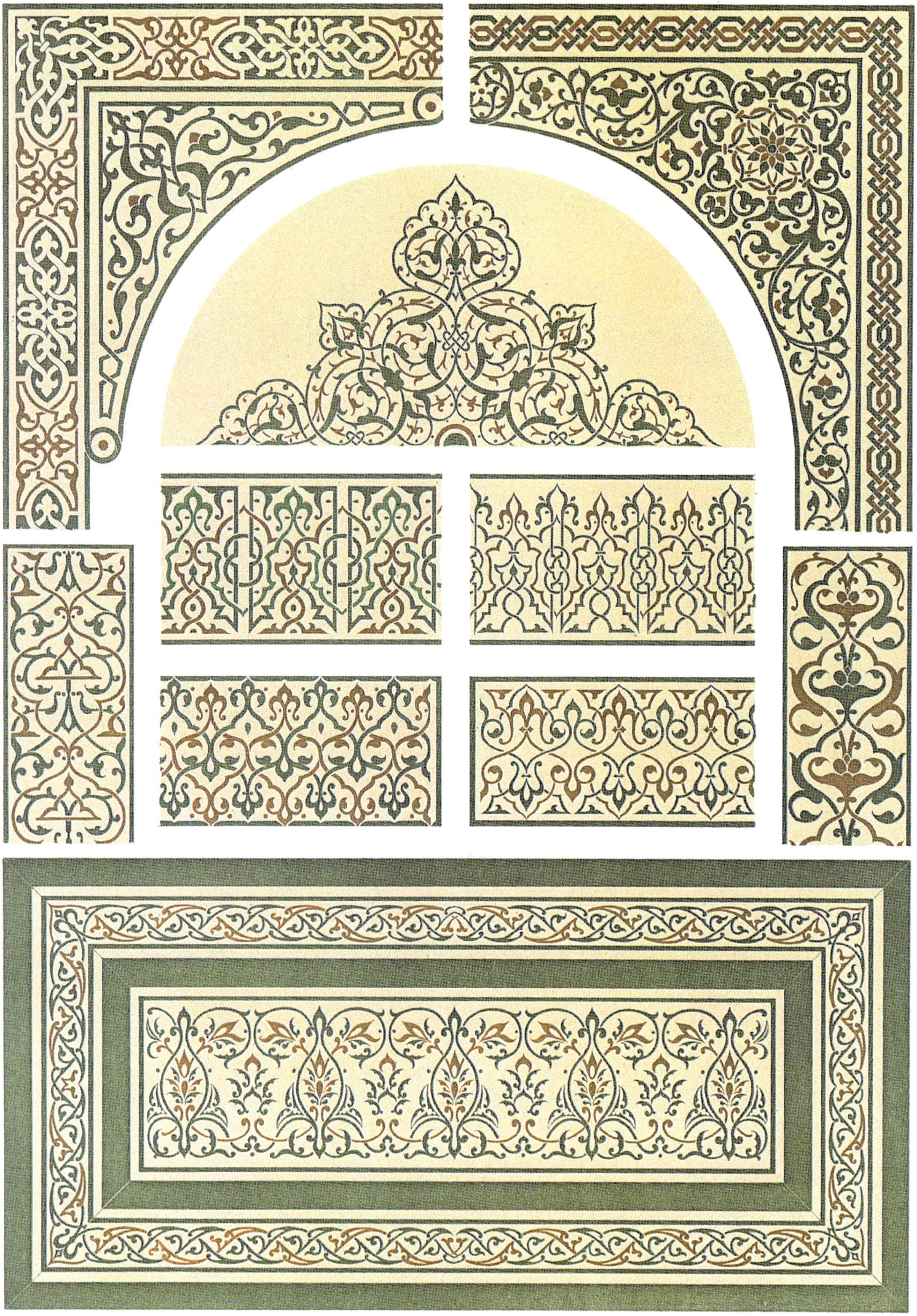

Stucco inlays on white marble (16th through 18th centuries).

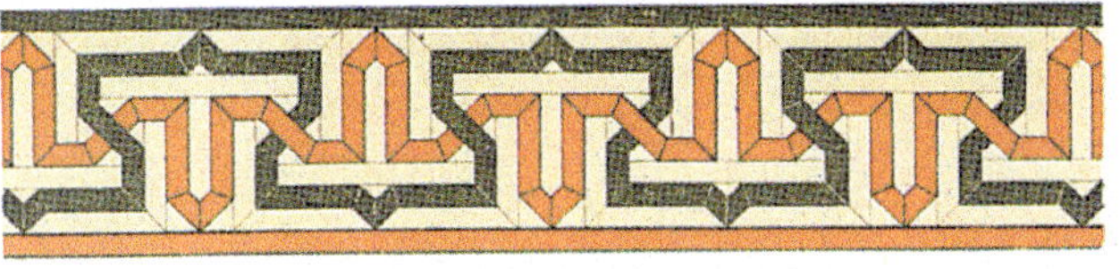

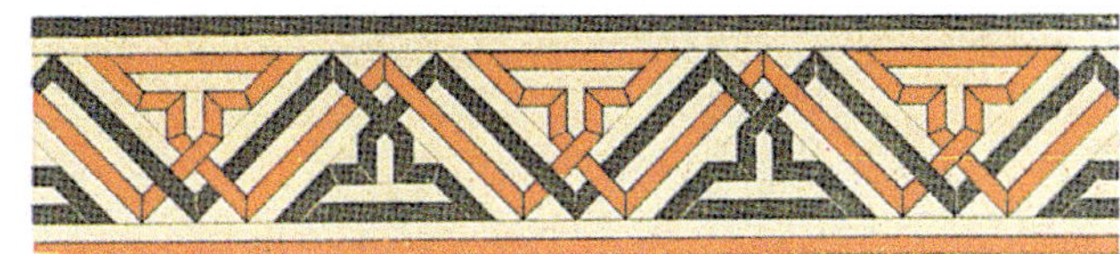

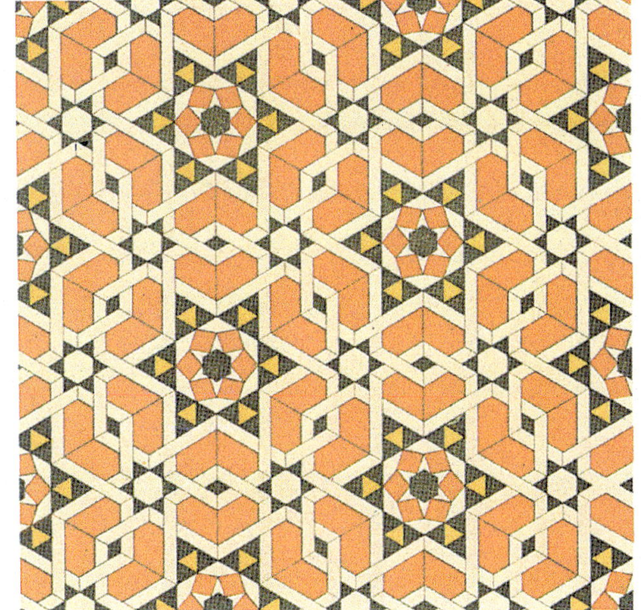

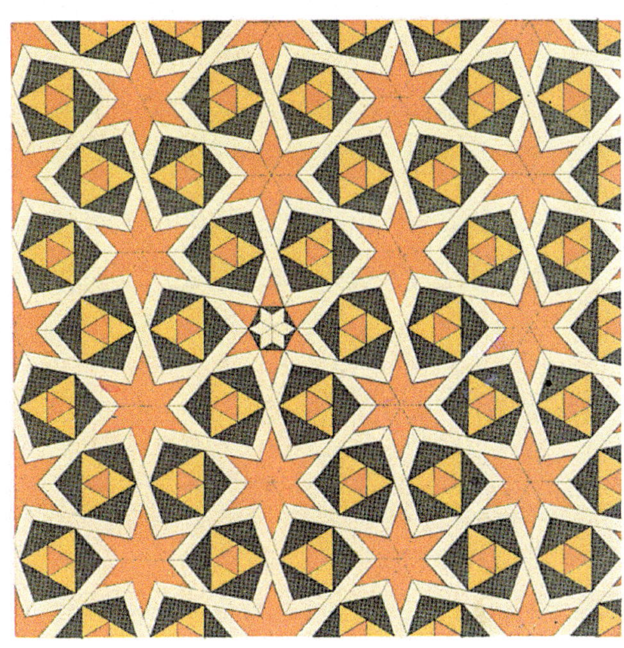

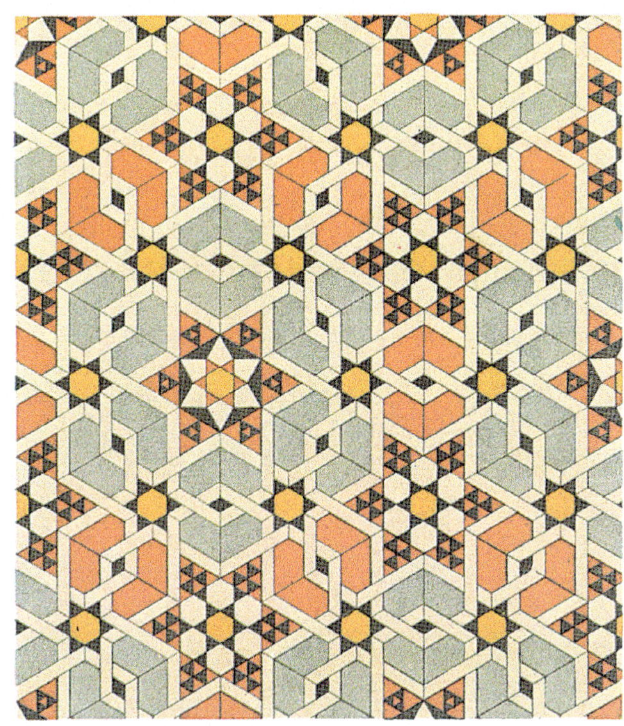

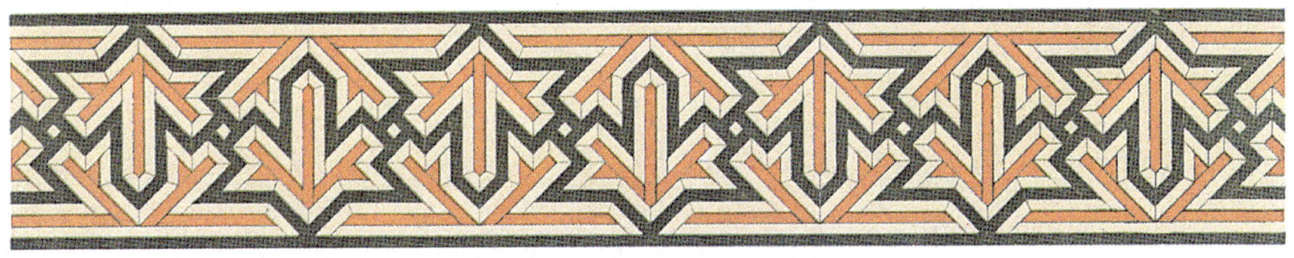

Wall mosaics (15th & 16th centuries).

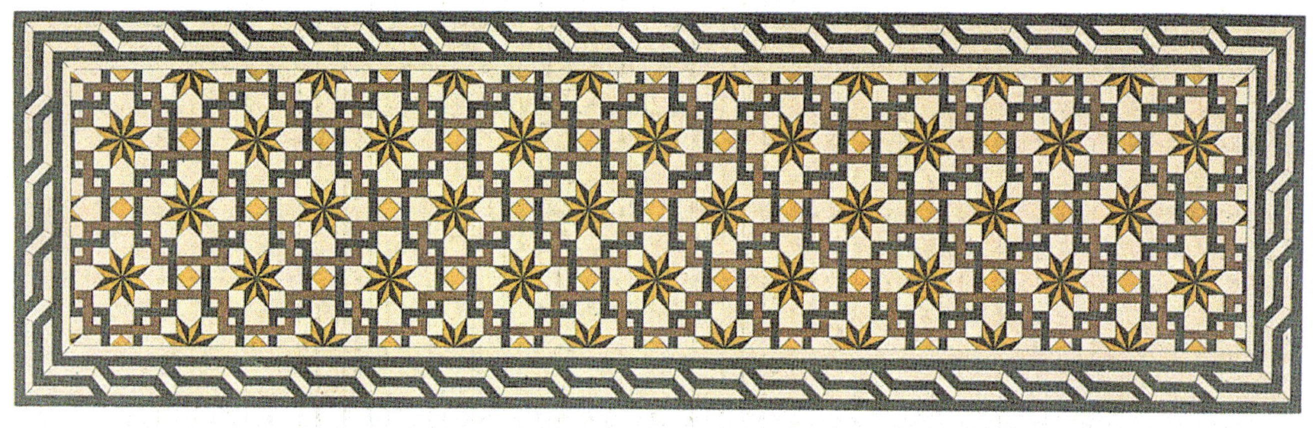

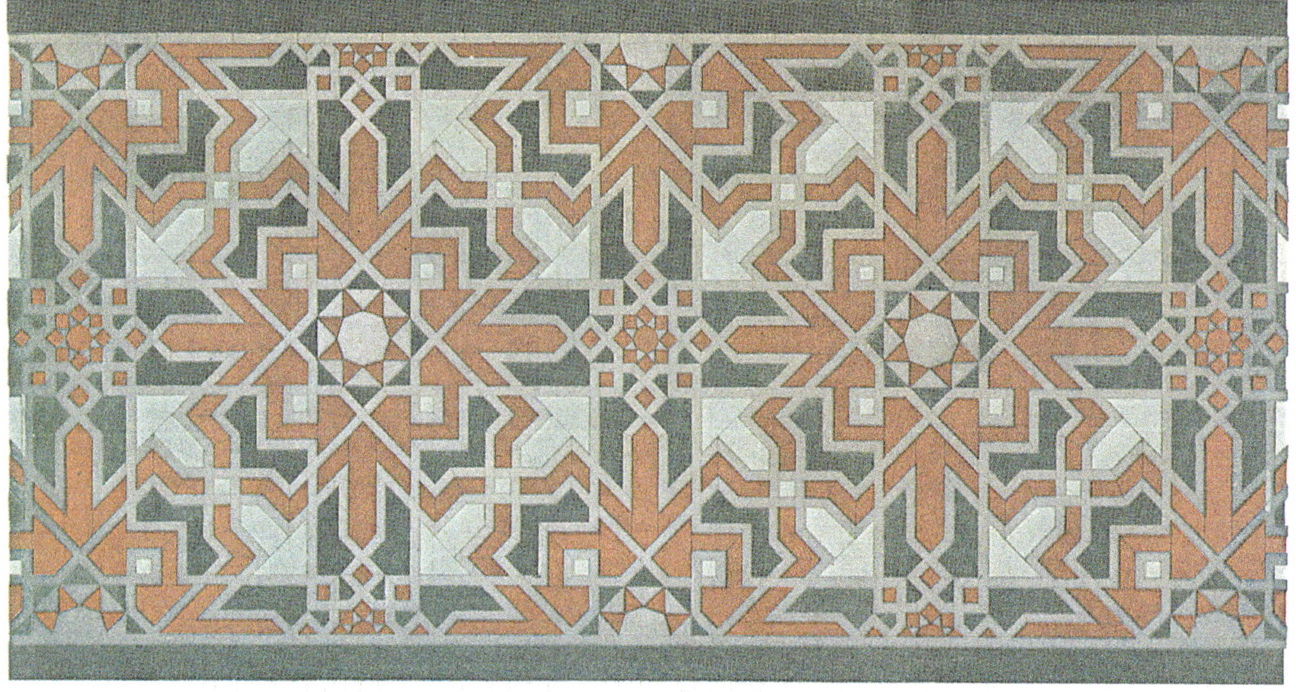

4   Details of wall mosaics in the mosque of Ahmed el-Bordeyny (17th century).

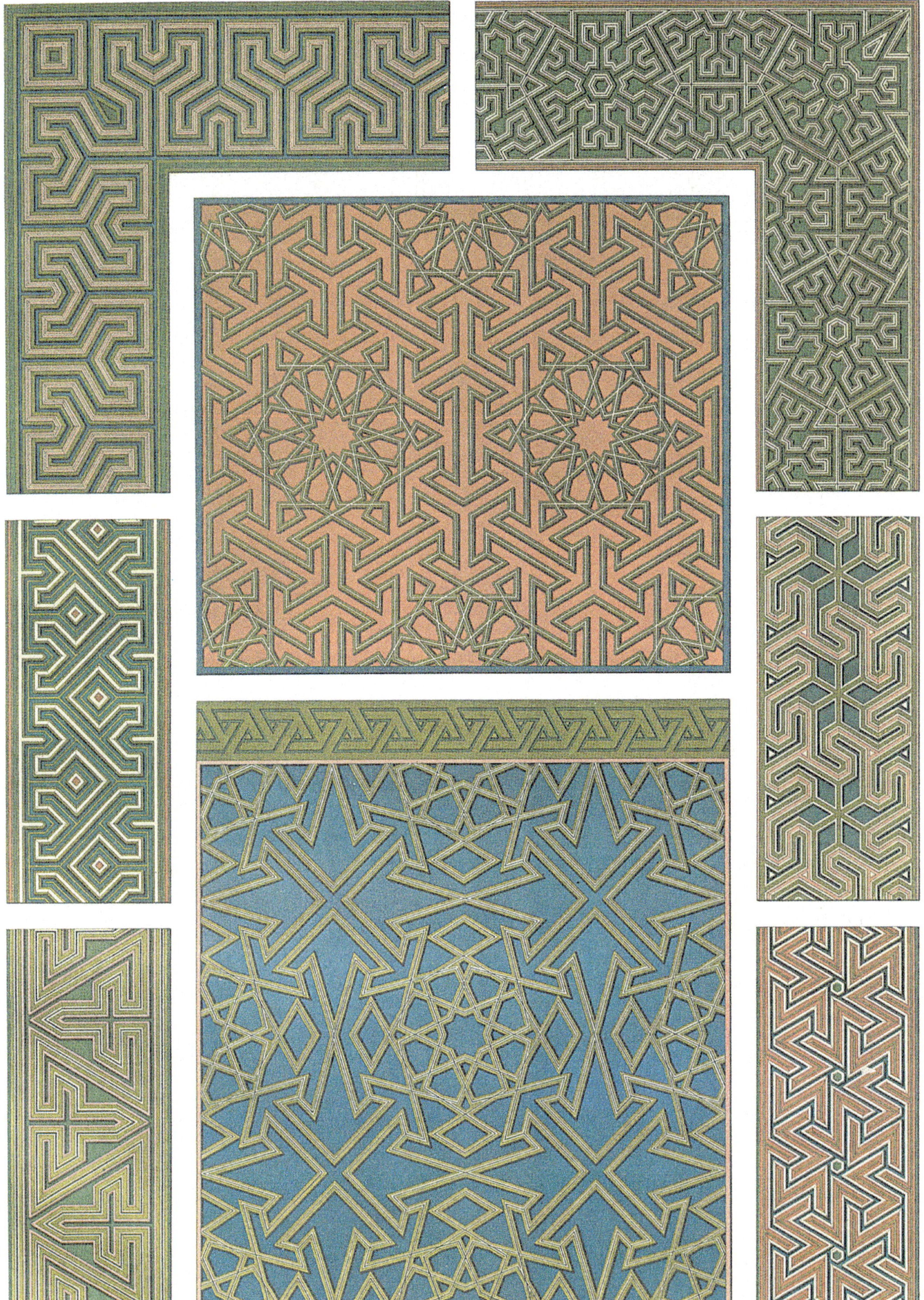

Panels and borders with carved-wood decoration.

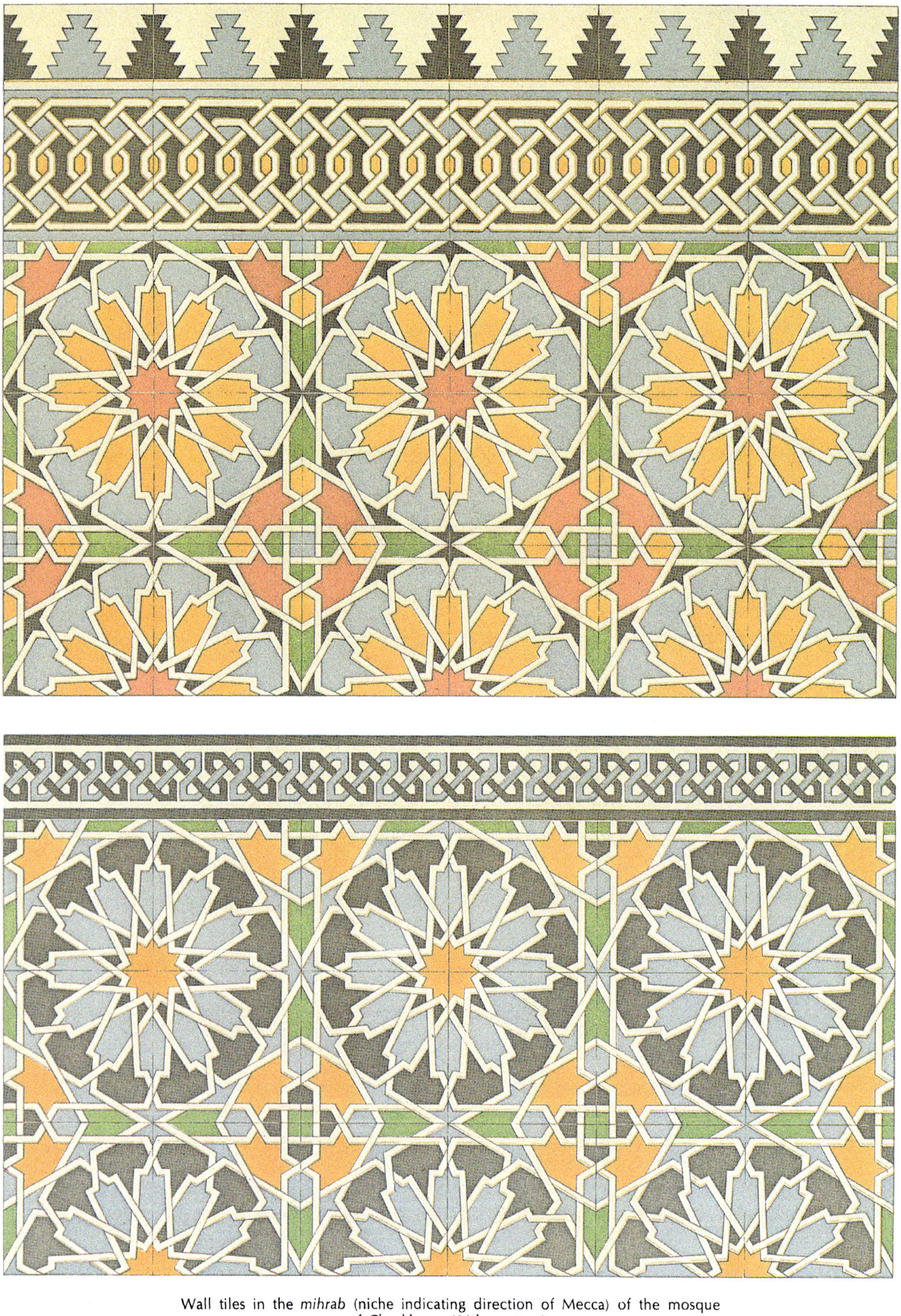

Wall tiles in the *mihrab* (niche indicating direction of Mecca) of the mosque
of Cheykhoun (14th century).

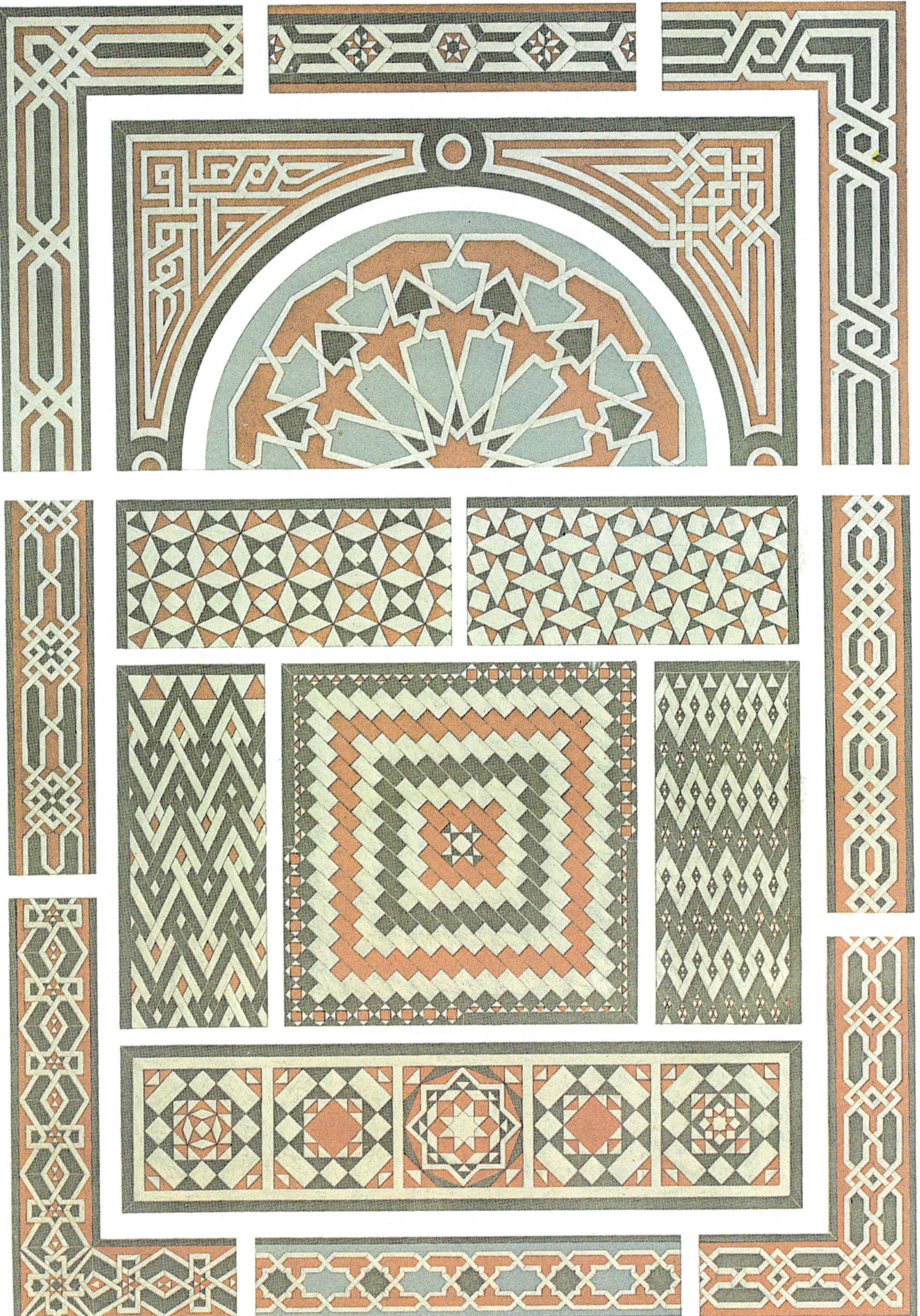

Details from mosaic facings and pavements (15th through 18th centuries).

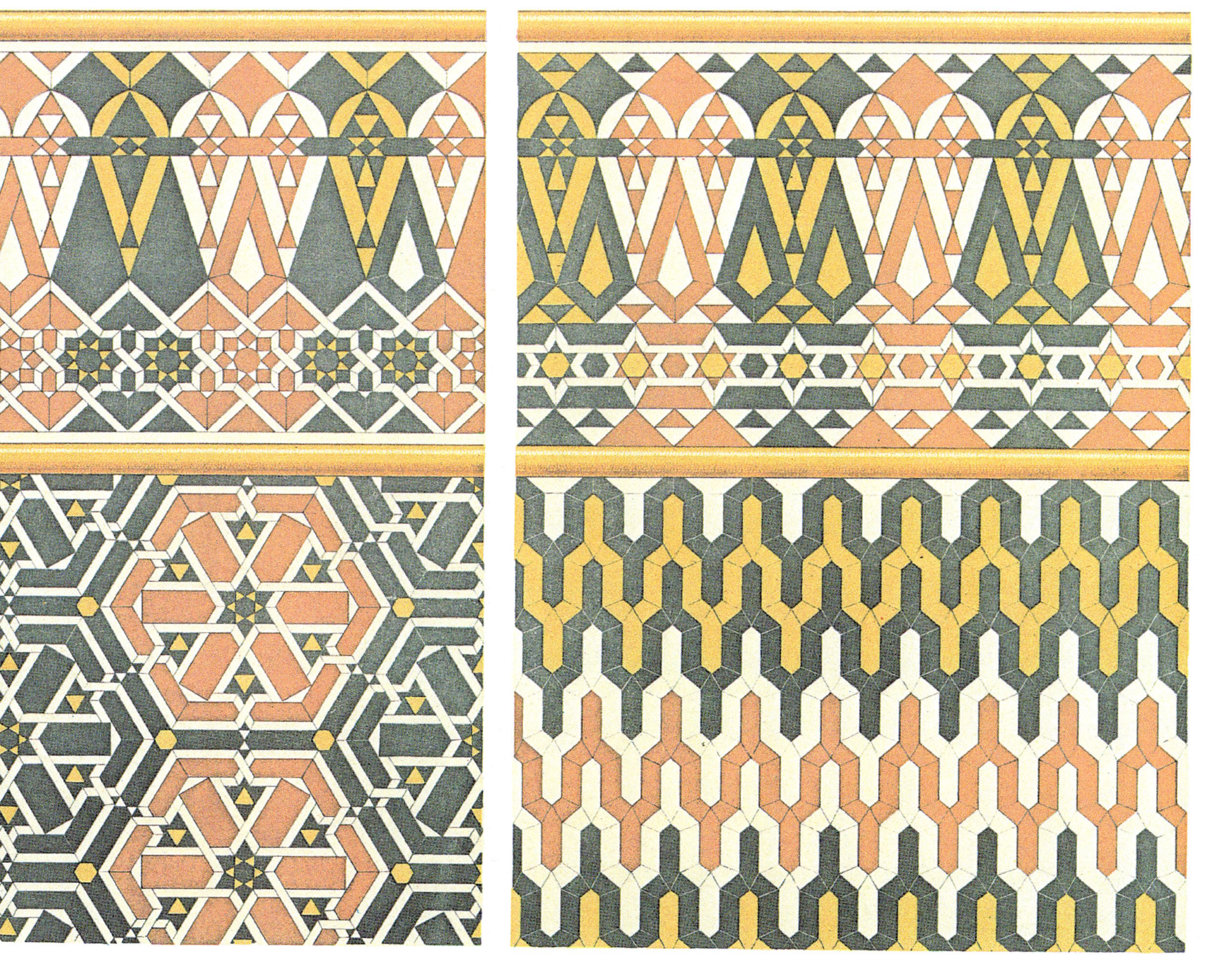

Wall mosaics (12th & 14th centuries).

8

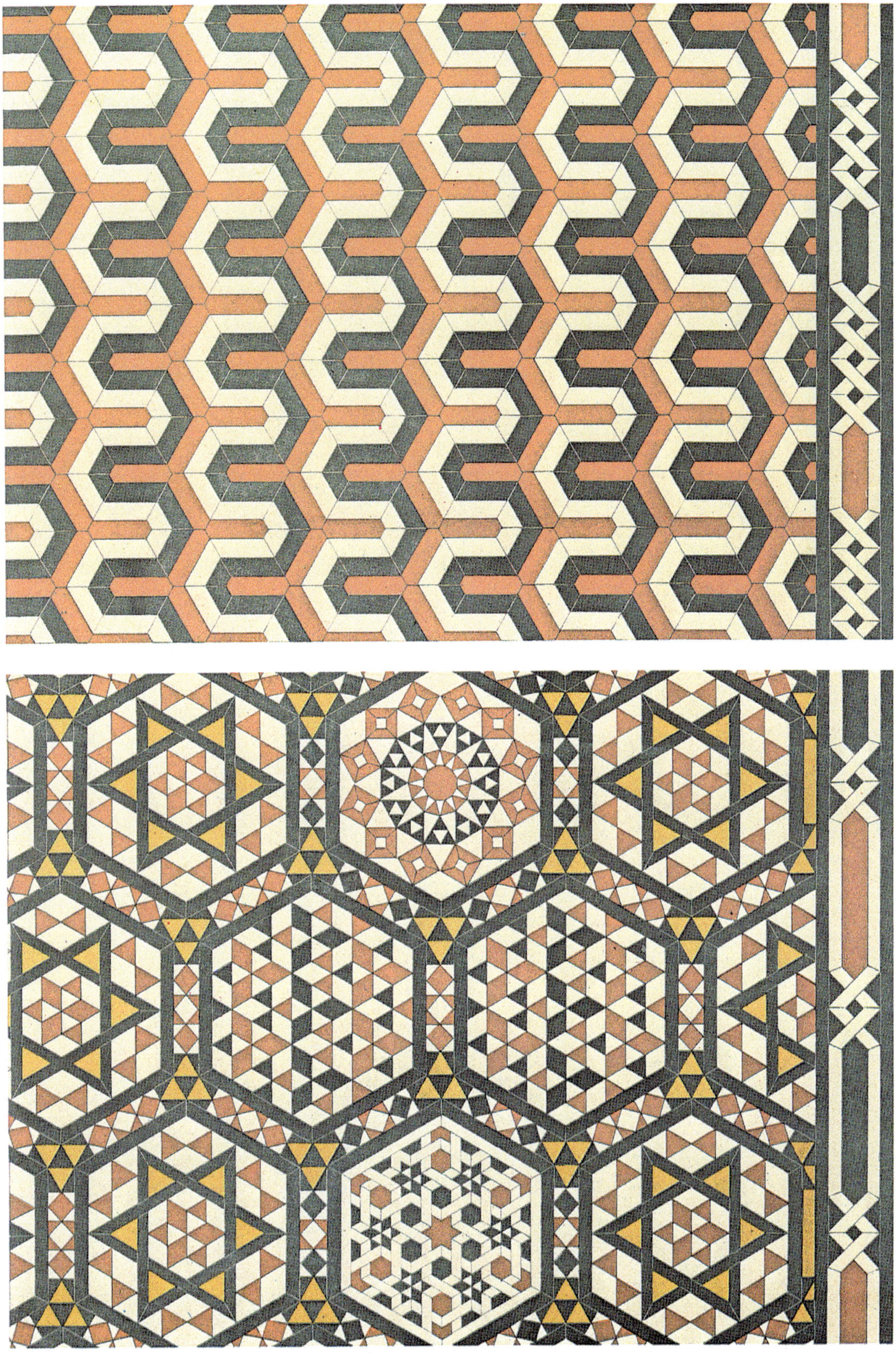

9

 Ceramic wall tiles from the Beyt el-Emyr (17th century).

Ceramic wall tiles: borders (16th century).

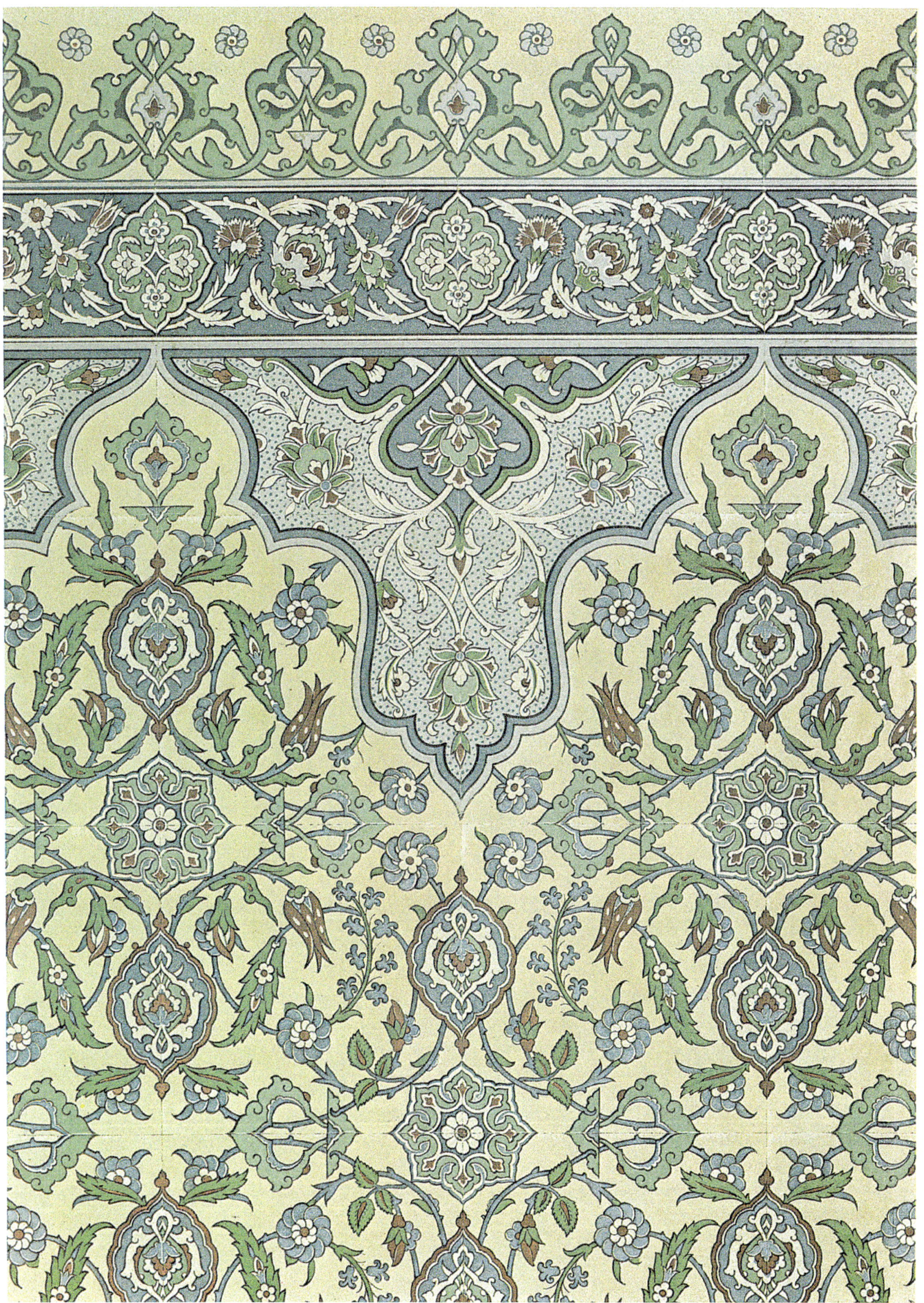

     Ceramic wall tiles from the Qasr Rodouan (16th century).

Ceramic wall tiles from the pavilion of Mahou Bey (16th century).   13

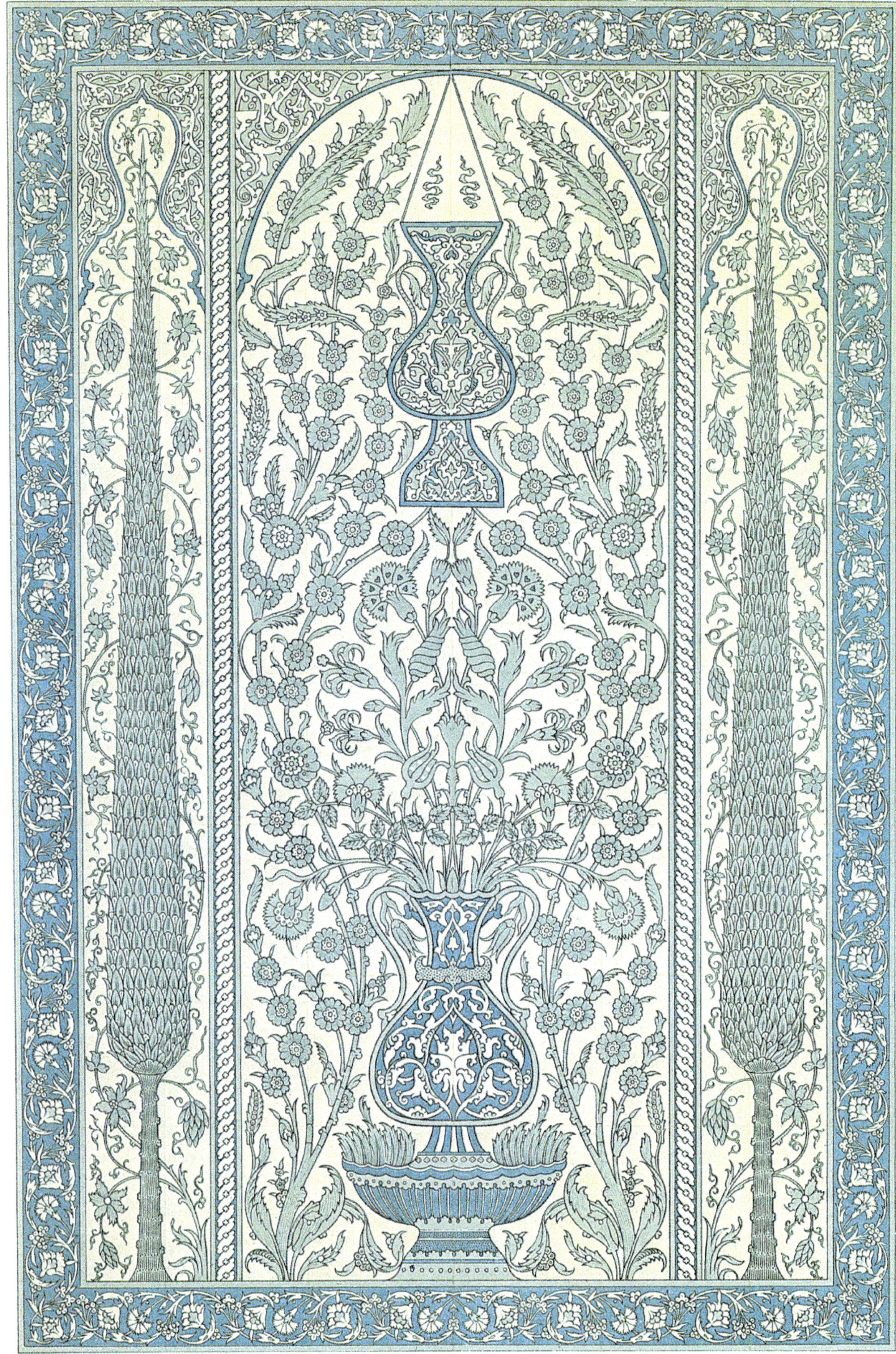

  Ceramic niche from the mosque of Ibrahym Agha (16th century).

Ceramic wall tiles from the mosque of Ibrahym Agha.

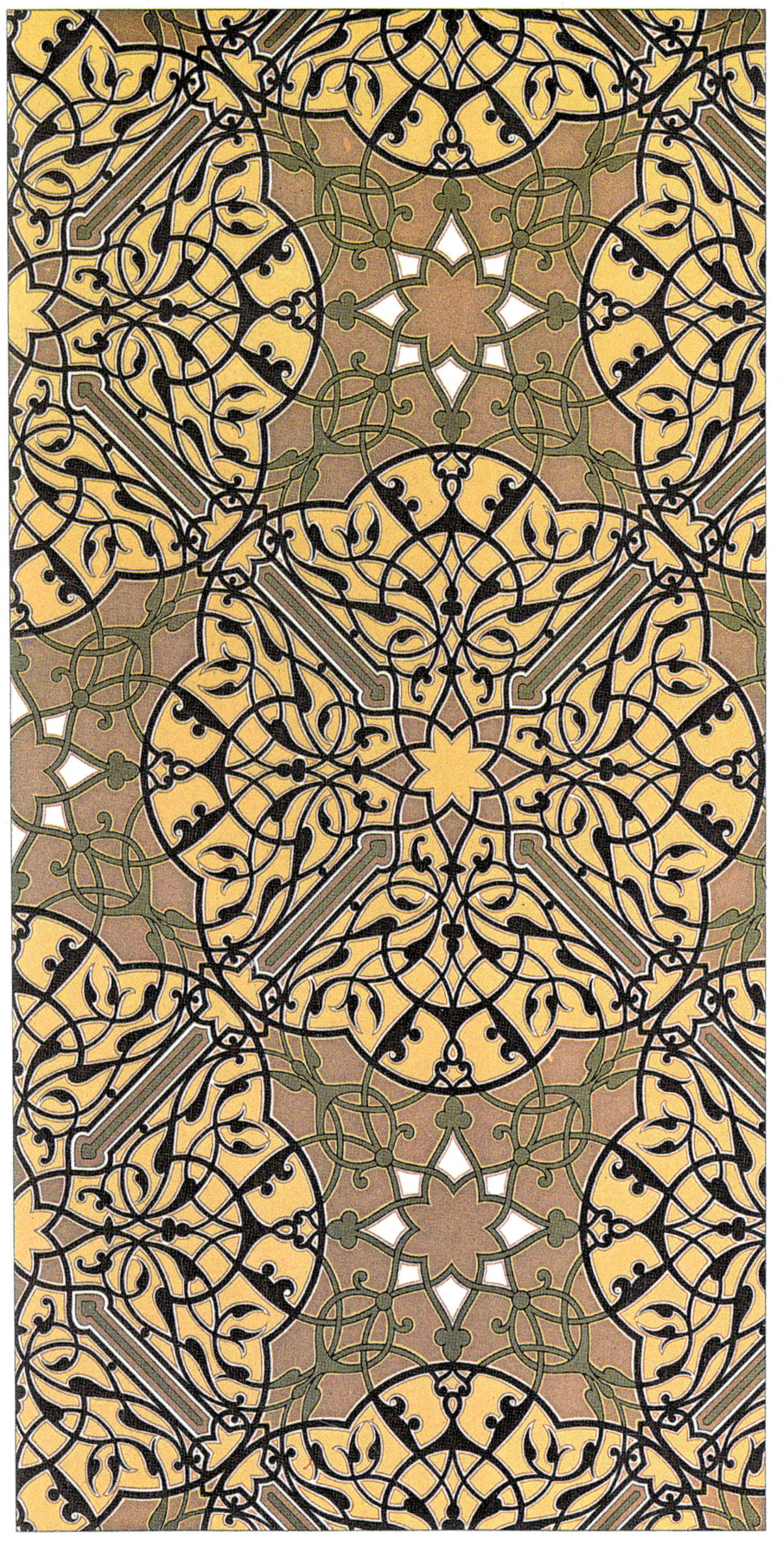

Ceiling areas in the mosque of Ahmed el-Bordeyny (17th century).

Ceiling area in the mosque of Ahmed el-Bordeyny.

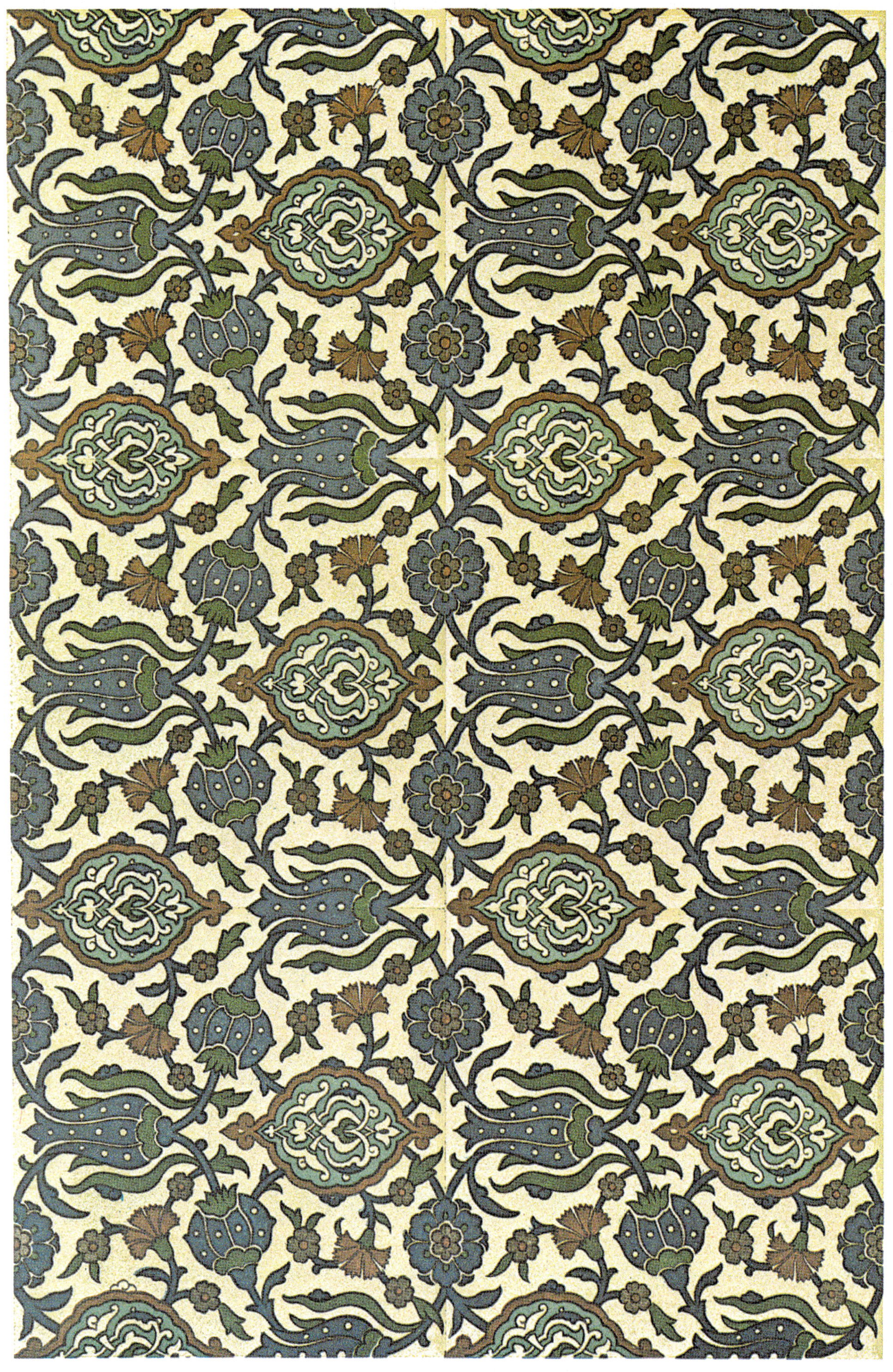

Ceramic wall tiles from a *hanout* (mortuary).

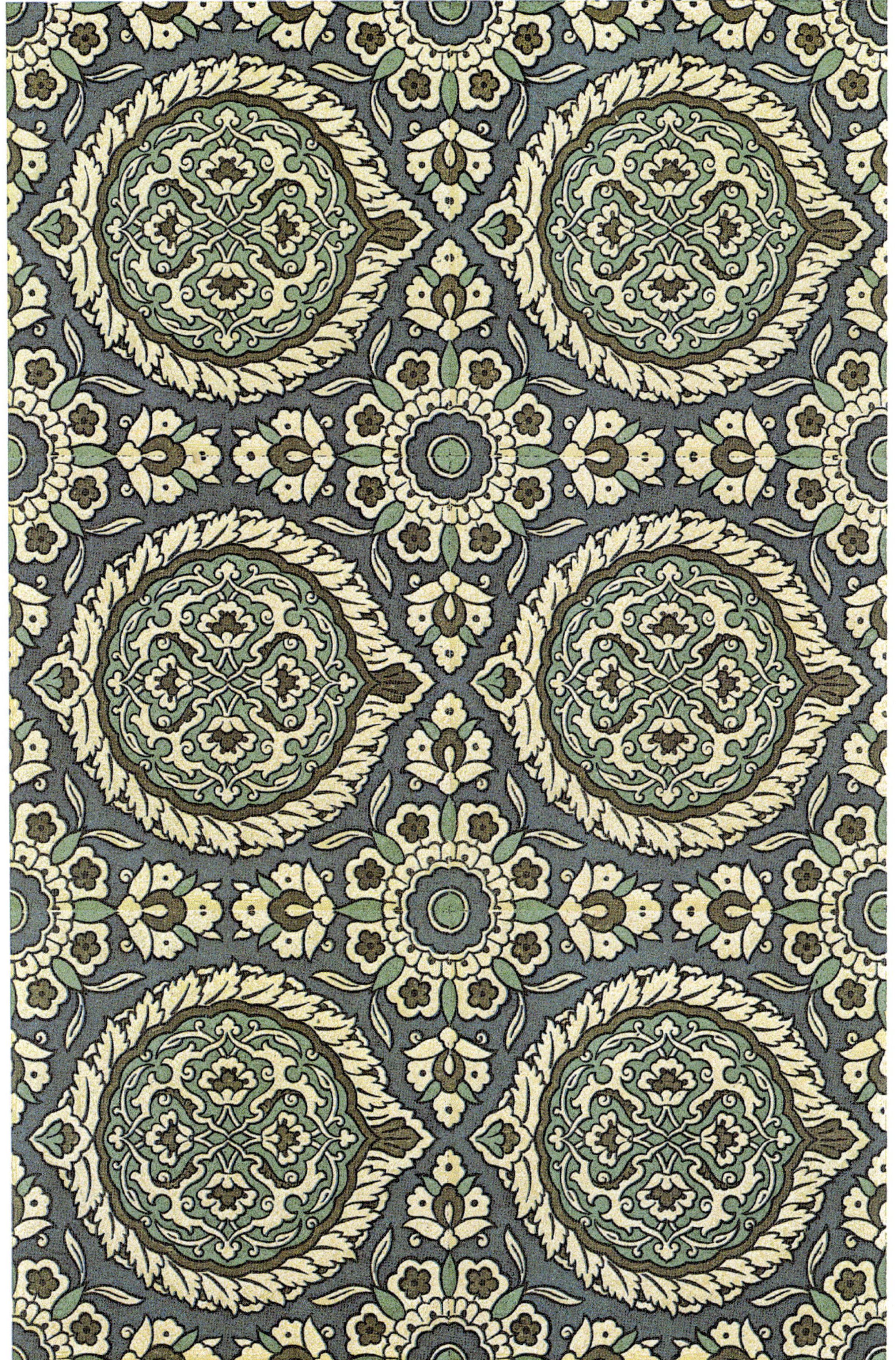

Ceramic wall tiles from a *hanout*.

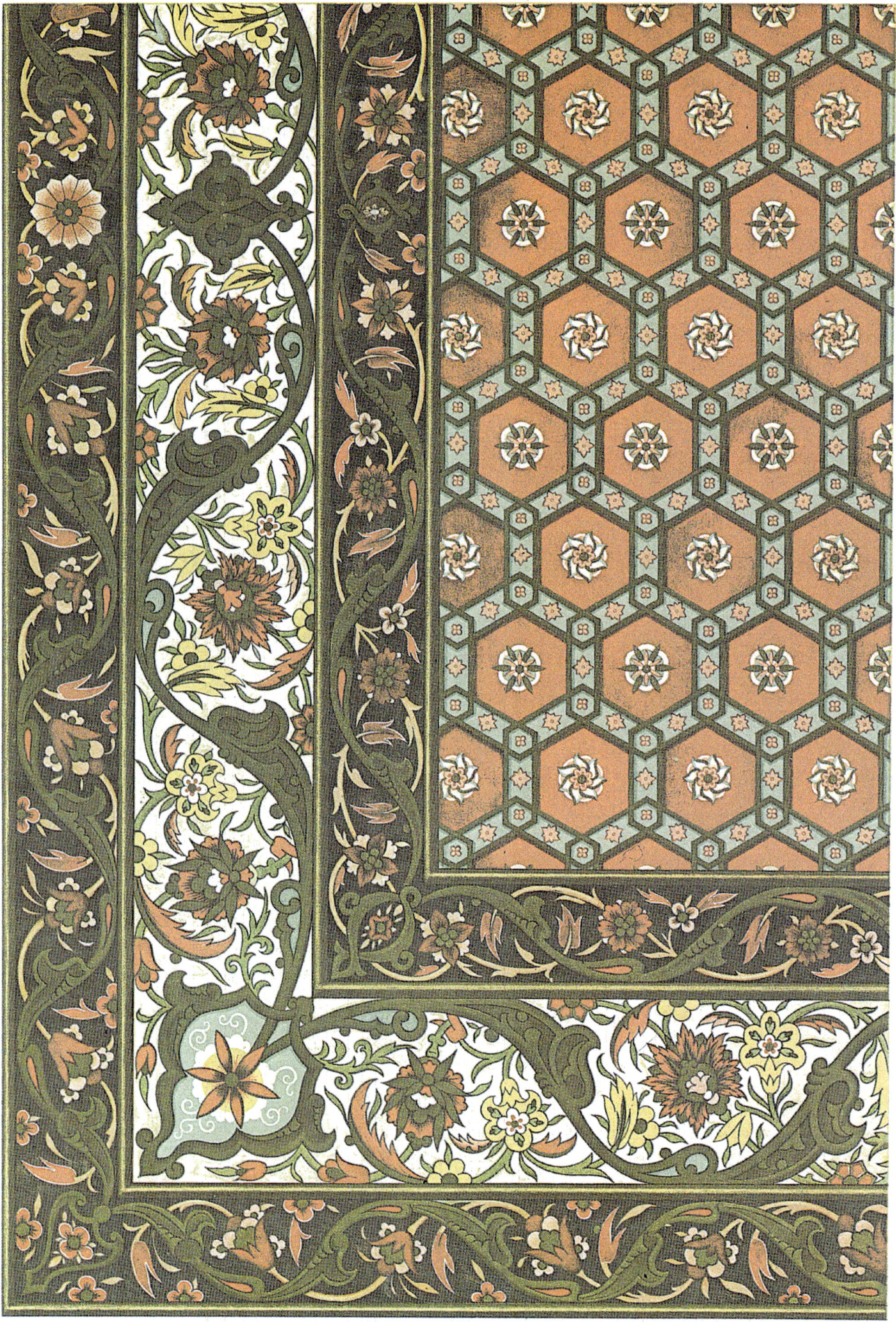

20 Detail from a ceiling (18th century).

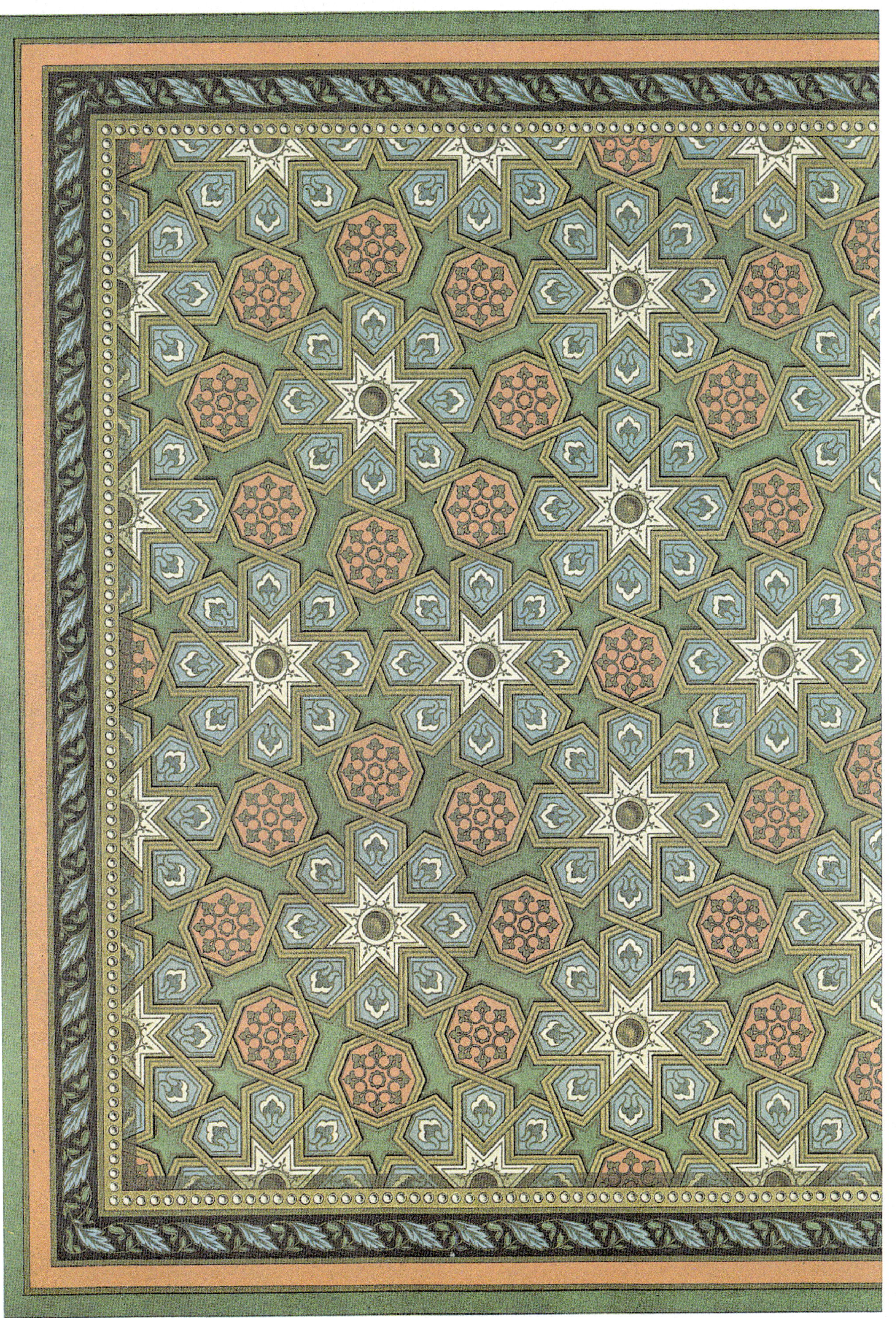

Ceiling design based on eight-pointed stars.

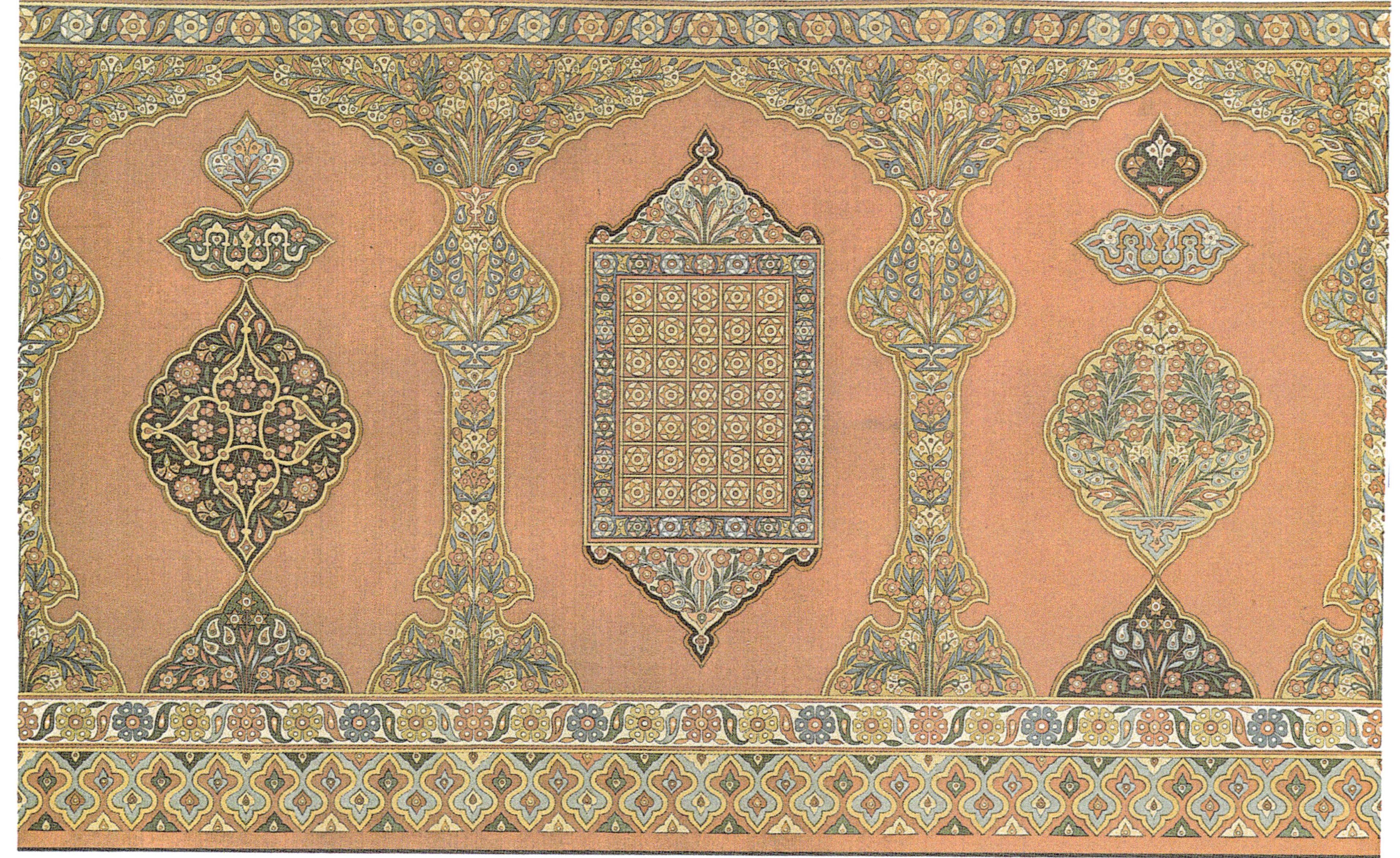

Design of a *heitha* (textile wall covering).

Ceiling from the Beyt el-Tchéléby (18th century).

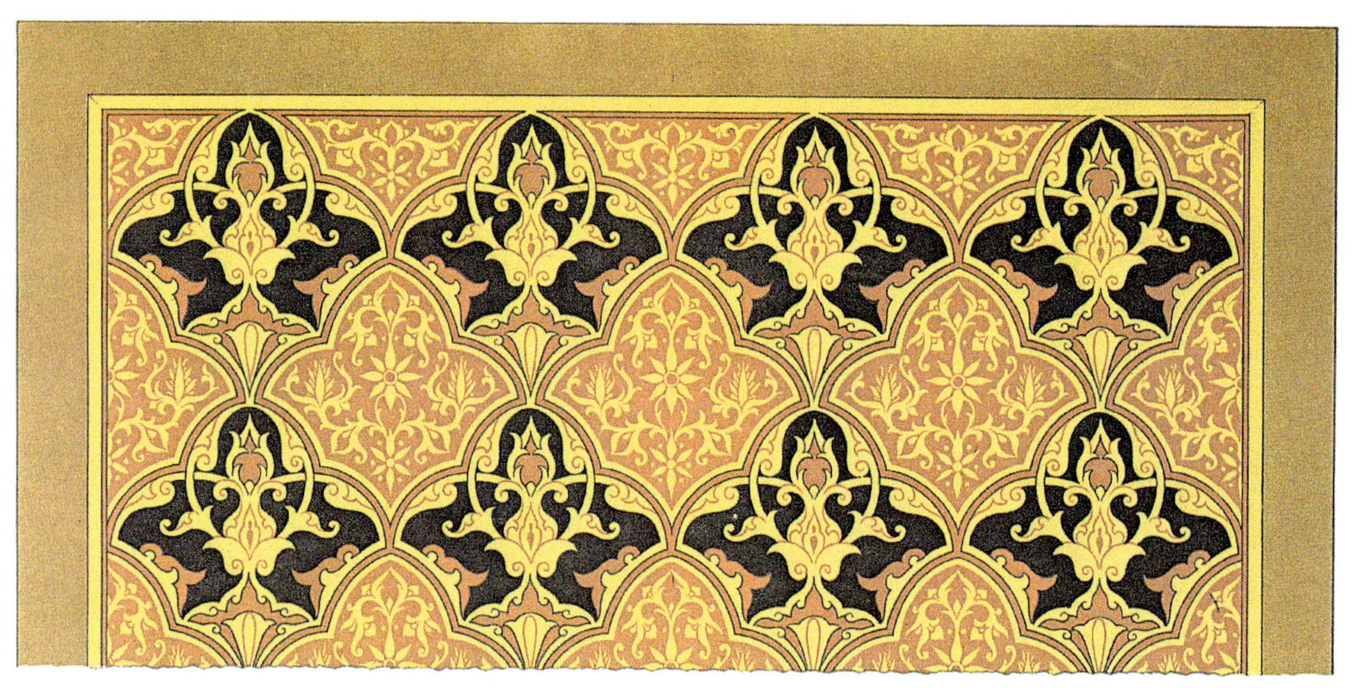

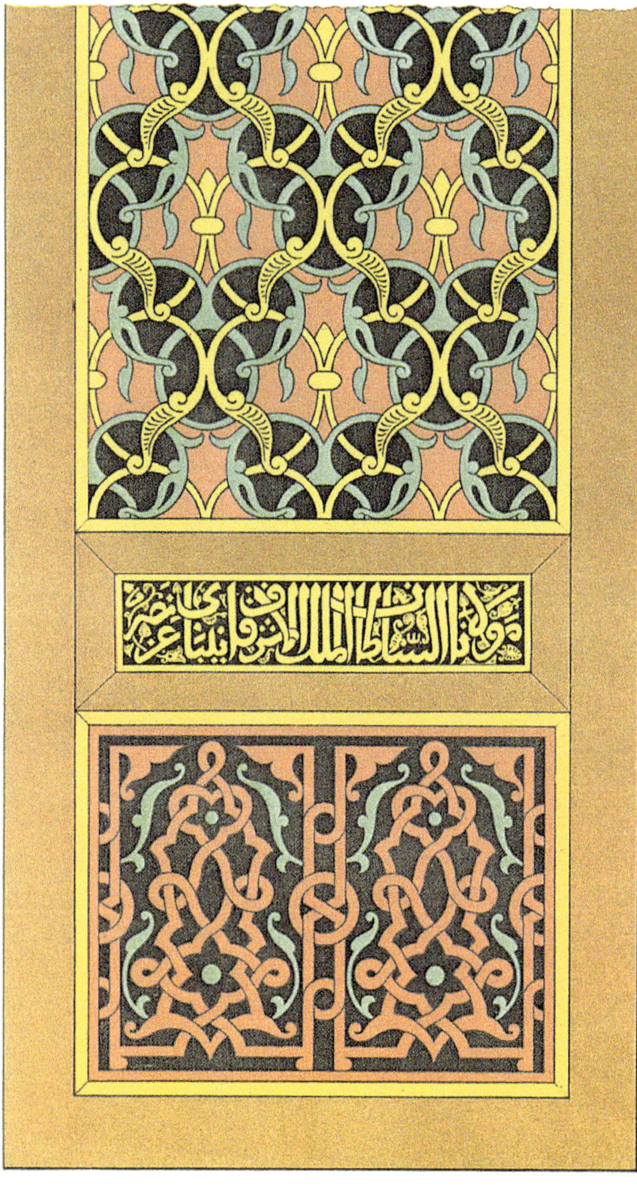

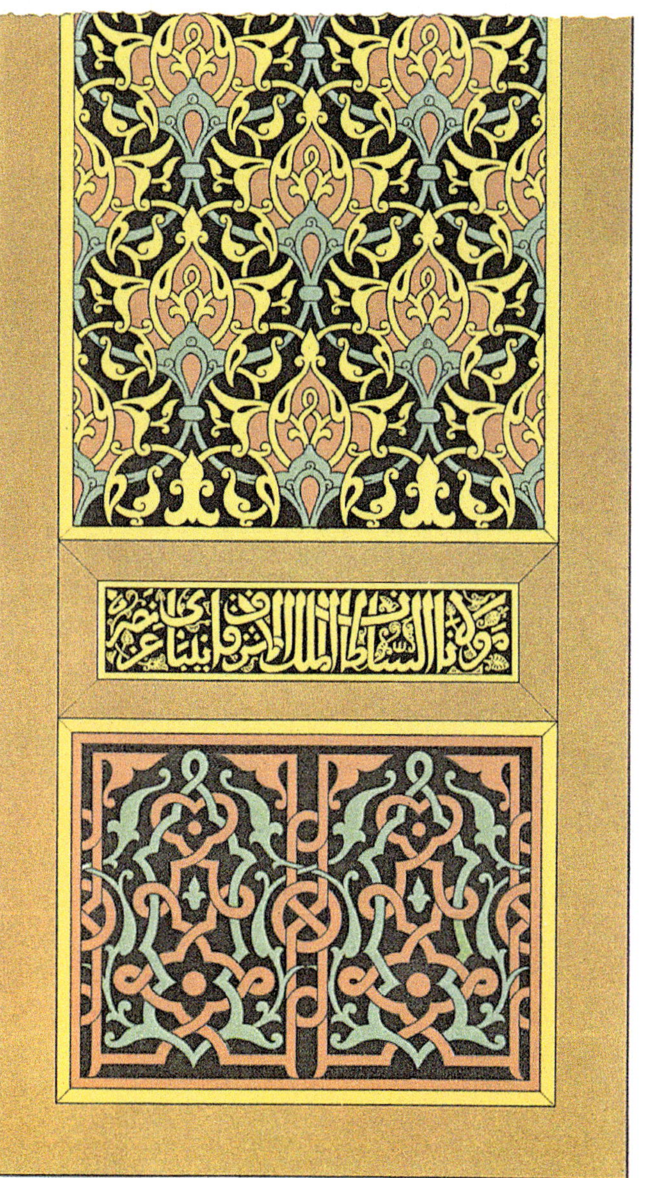

   Painted decorations of doors and cabinets in the mosque of Qaytbay (15th century).

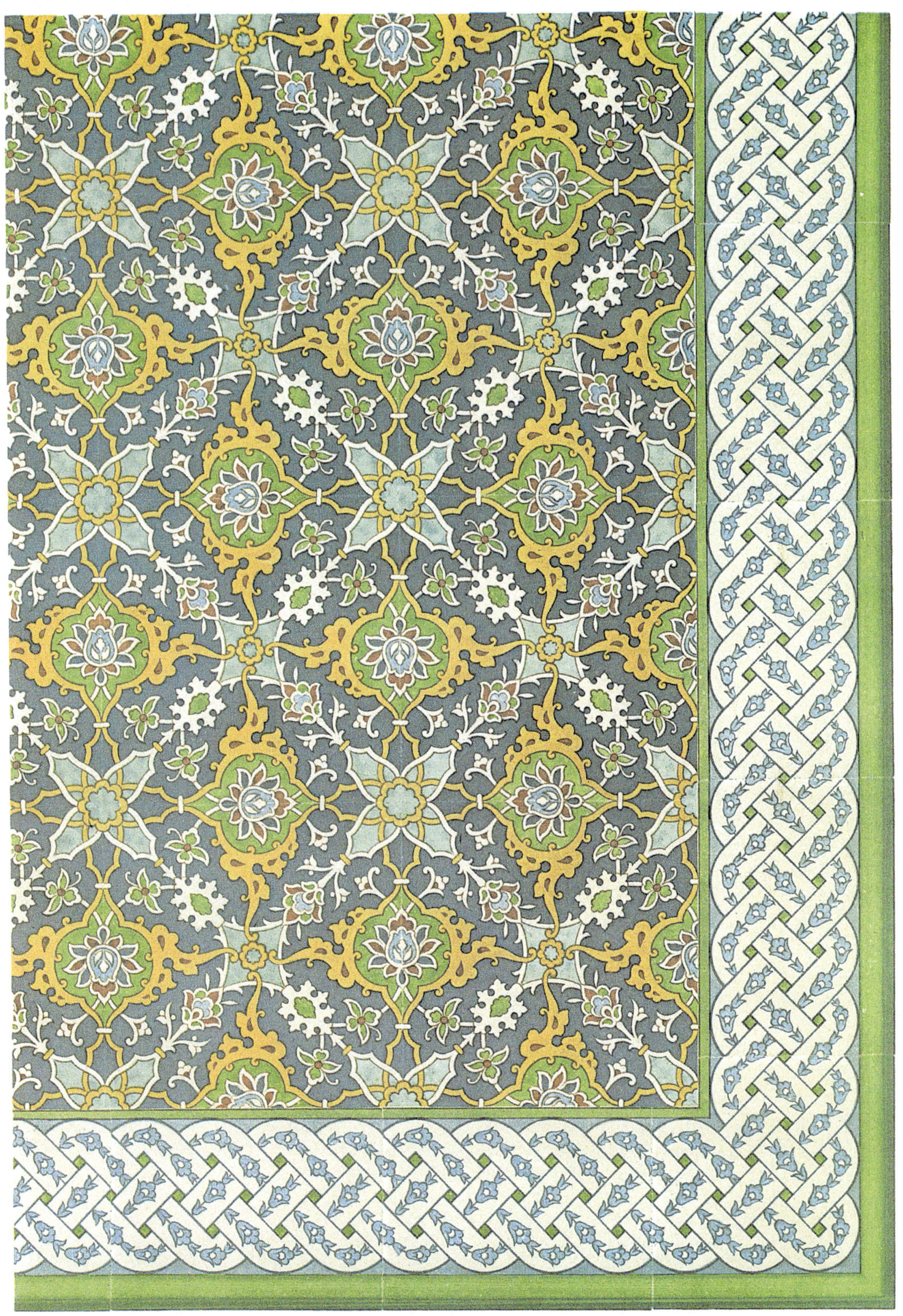

Ceramic wall tiles from the monastery of the Dervishes (17th century).

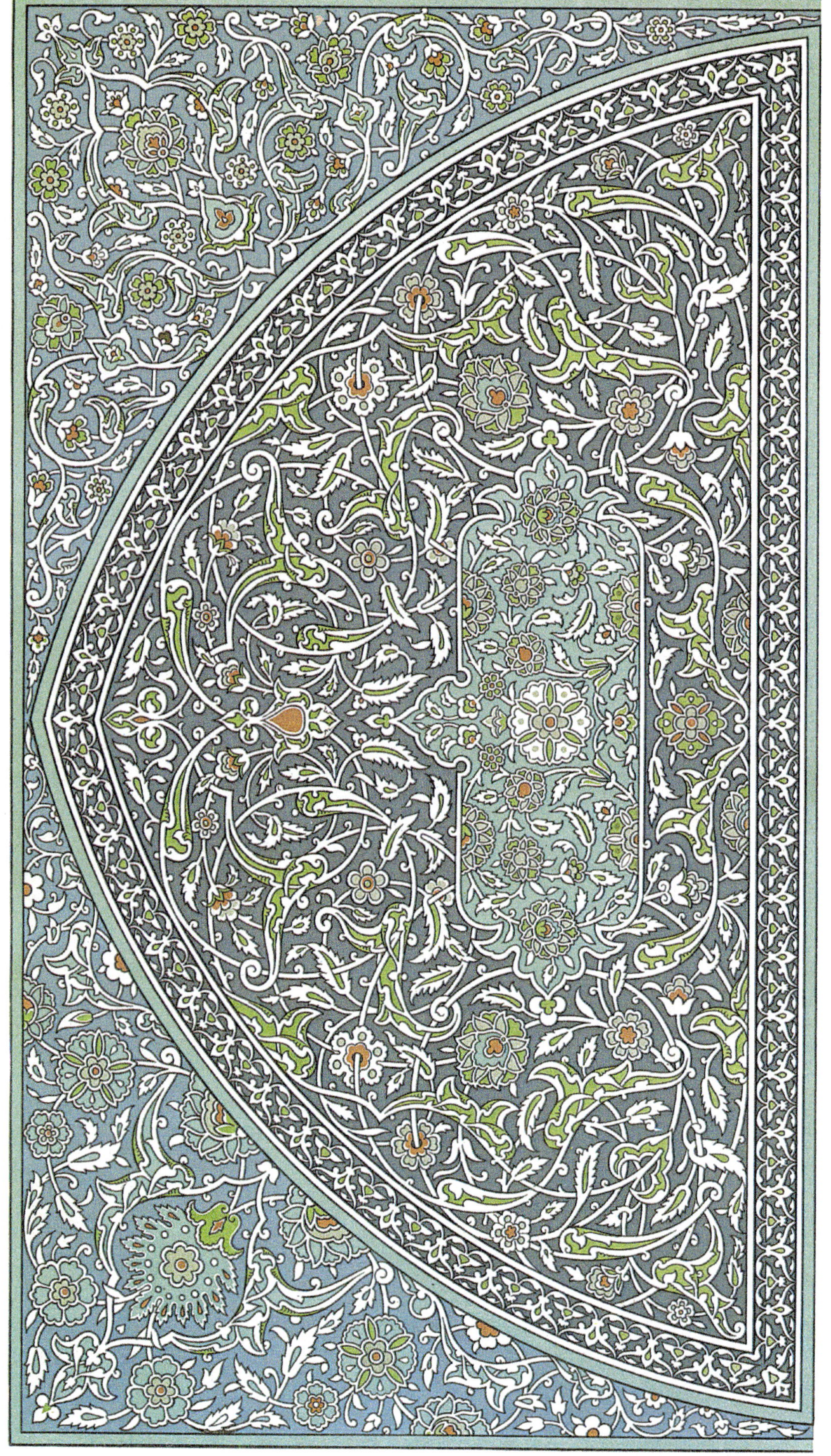

Ceramic tiles from the mosque/cathedral of Qous: tympanum and spandrels (16th century).

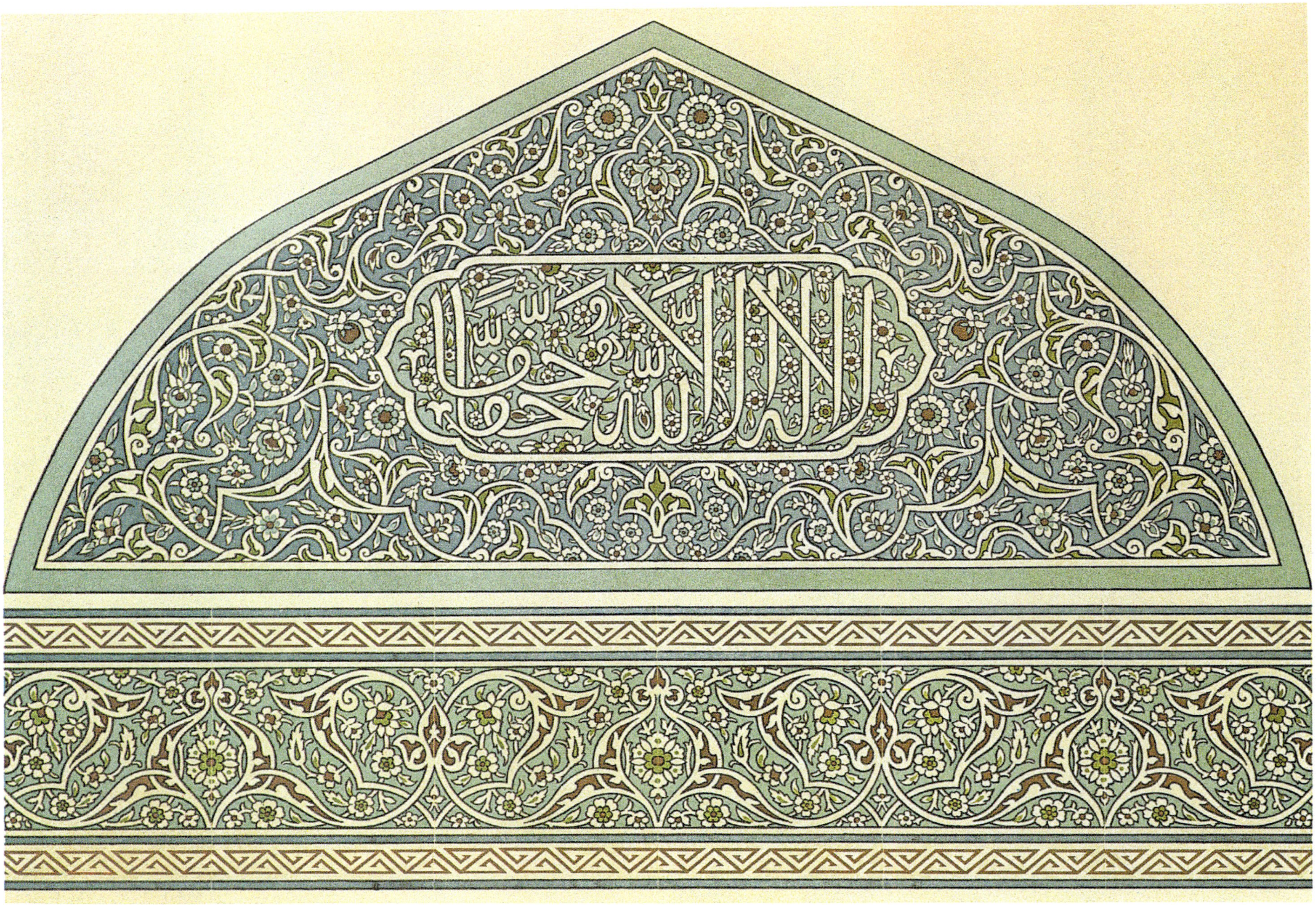

Enameled tile tympanum and border from an arcade of the monastery of the
Dervishes (17th century).

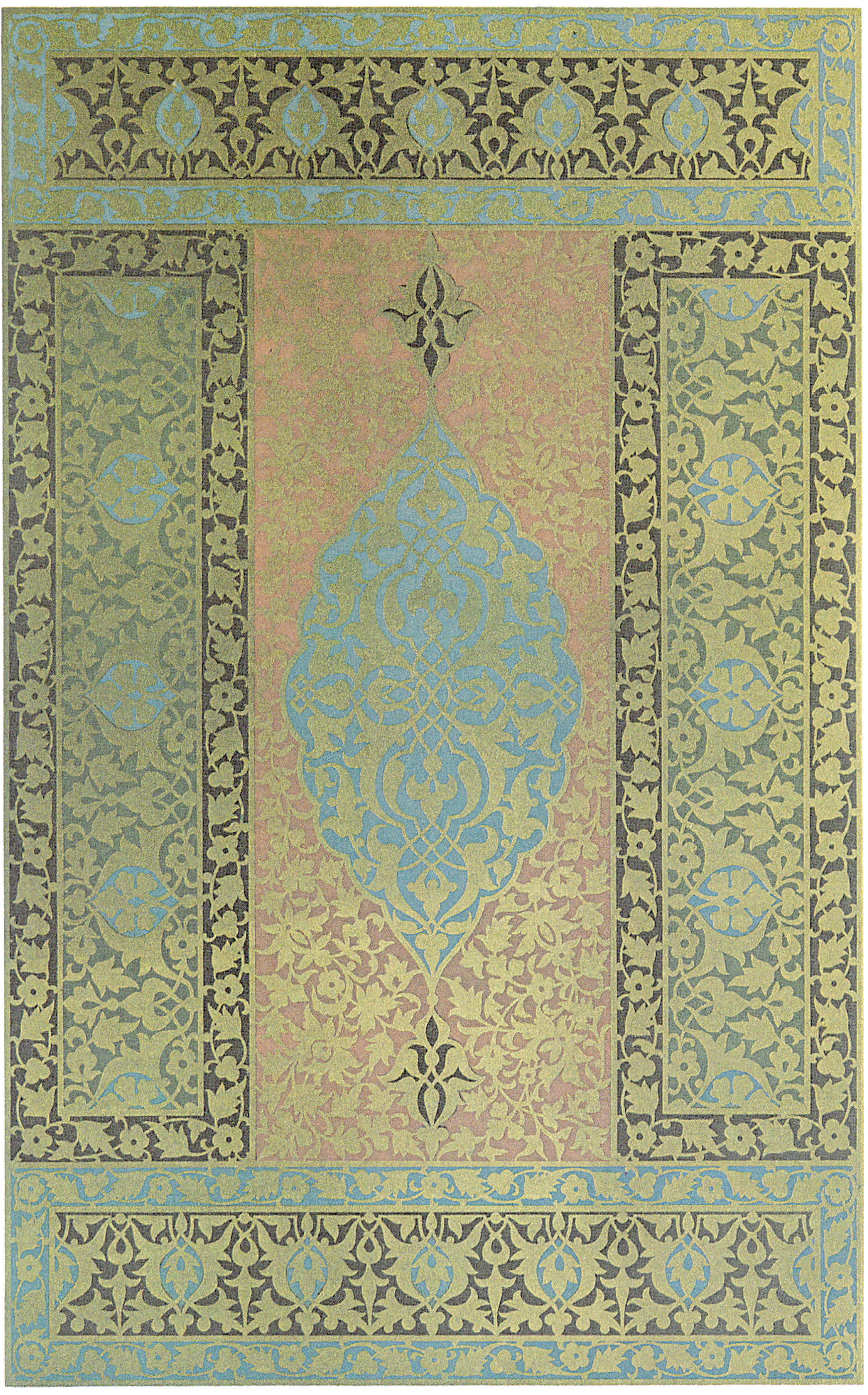

   Cut-out and appliquéd paper, used as wall covering (18th century).

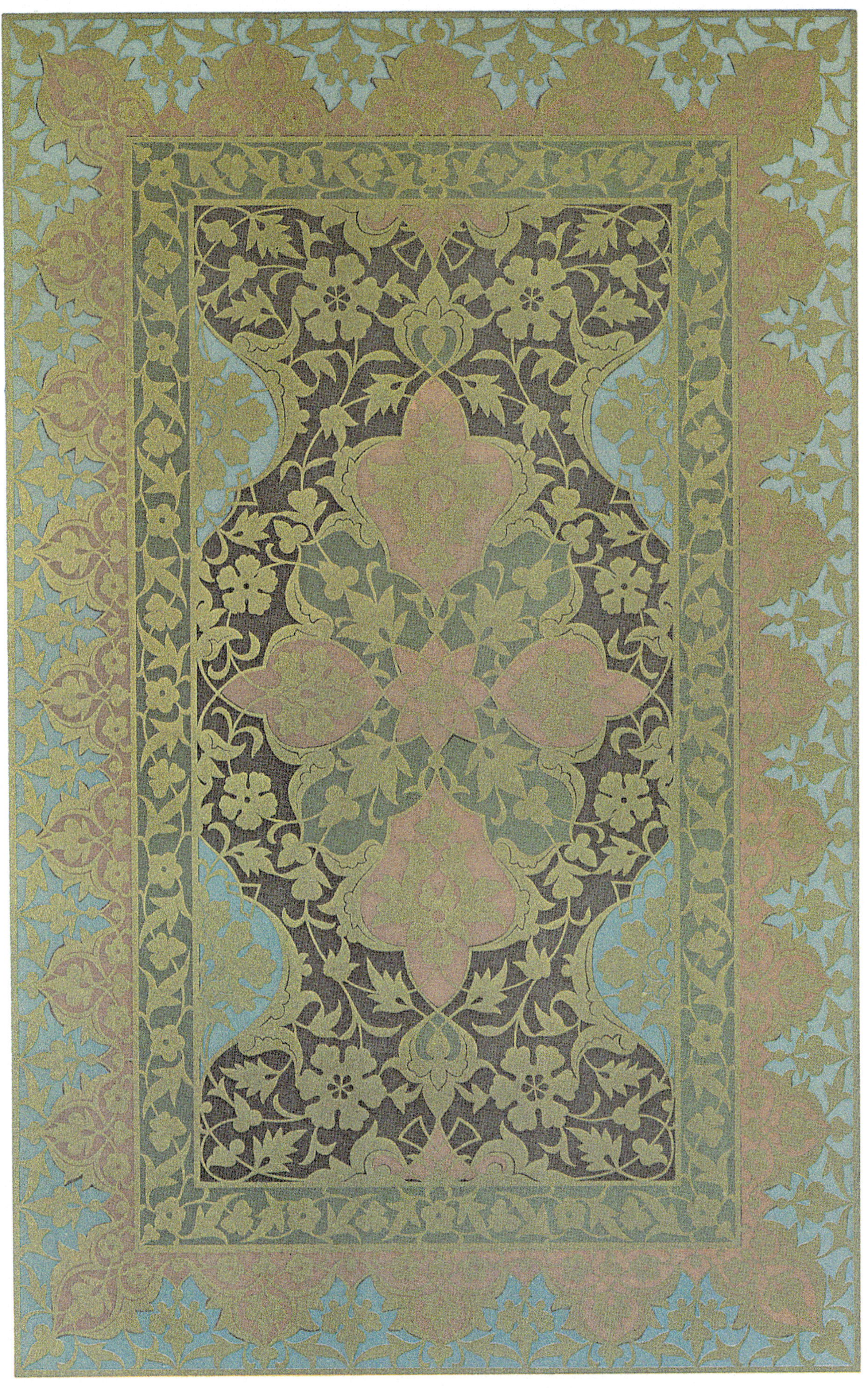

Cut-out and appliquéd paper, used as wall covering (18th century).

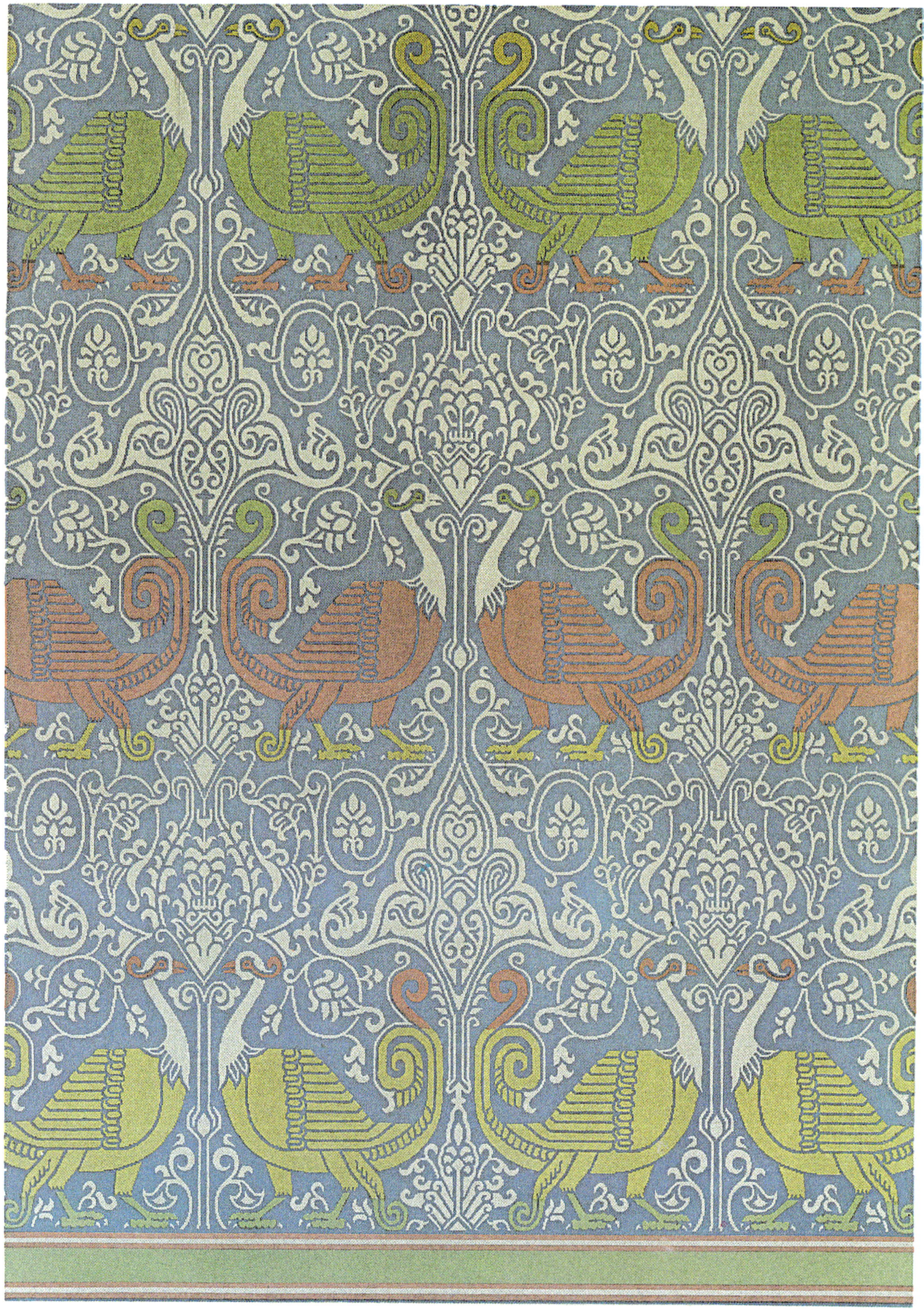

     Textile in a Utrecht (Netherlands) collection (14th century).

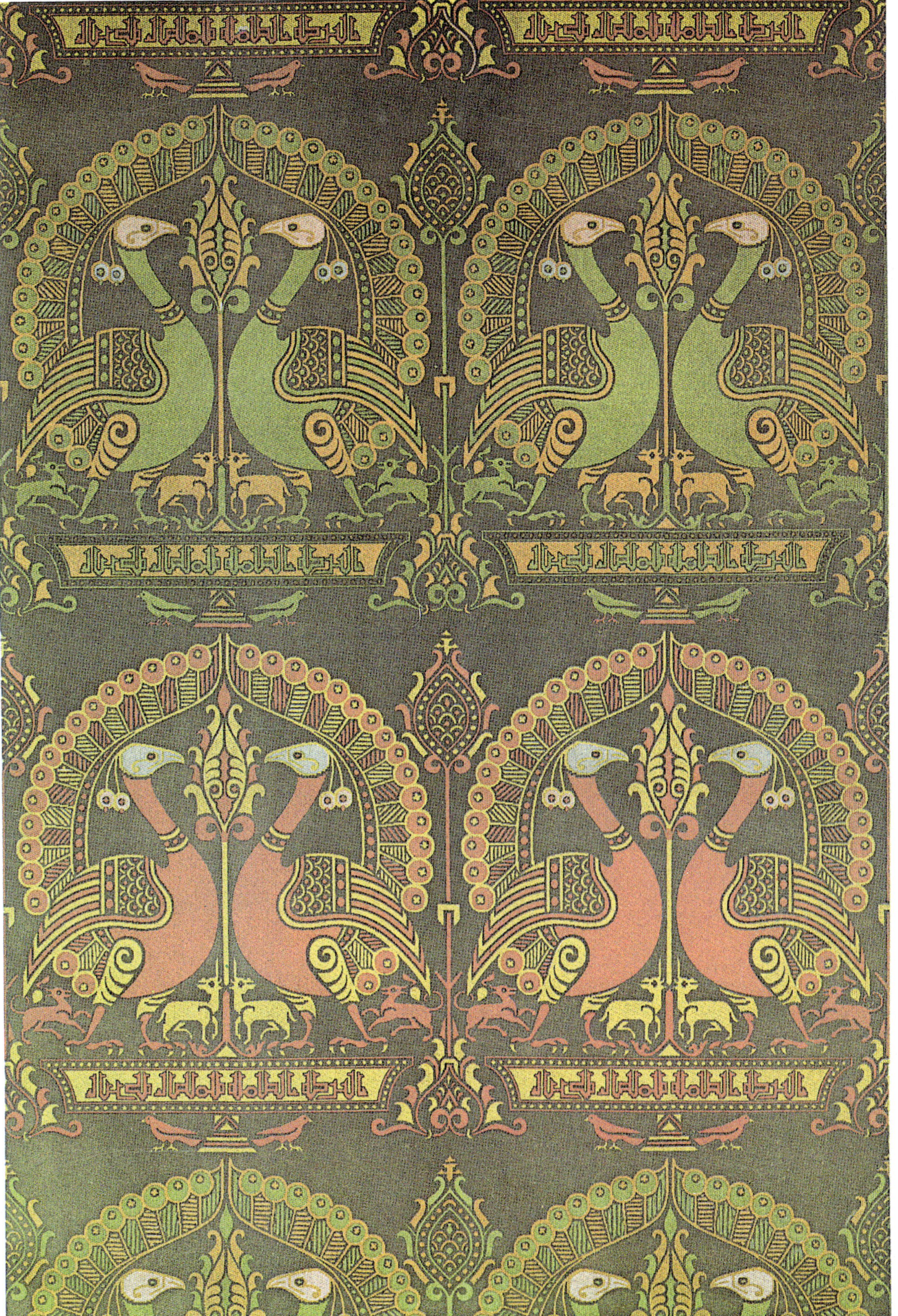

Silk textile in a Toulouse (France) collection (14th century).

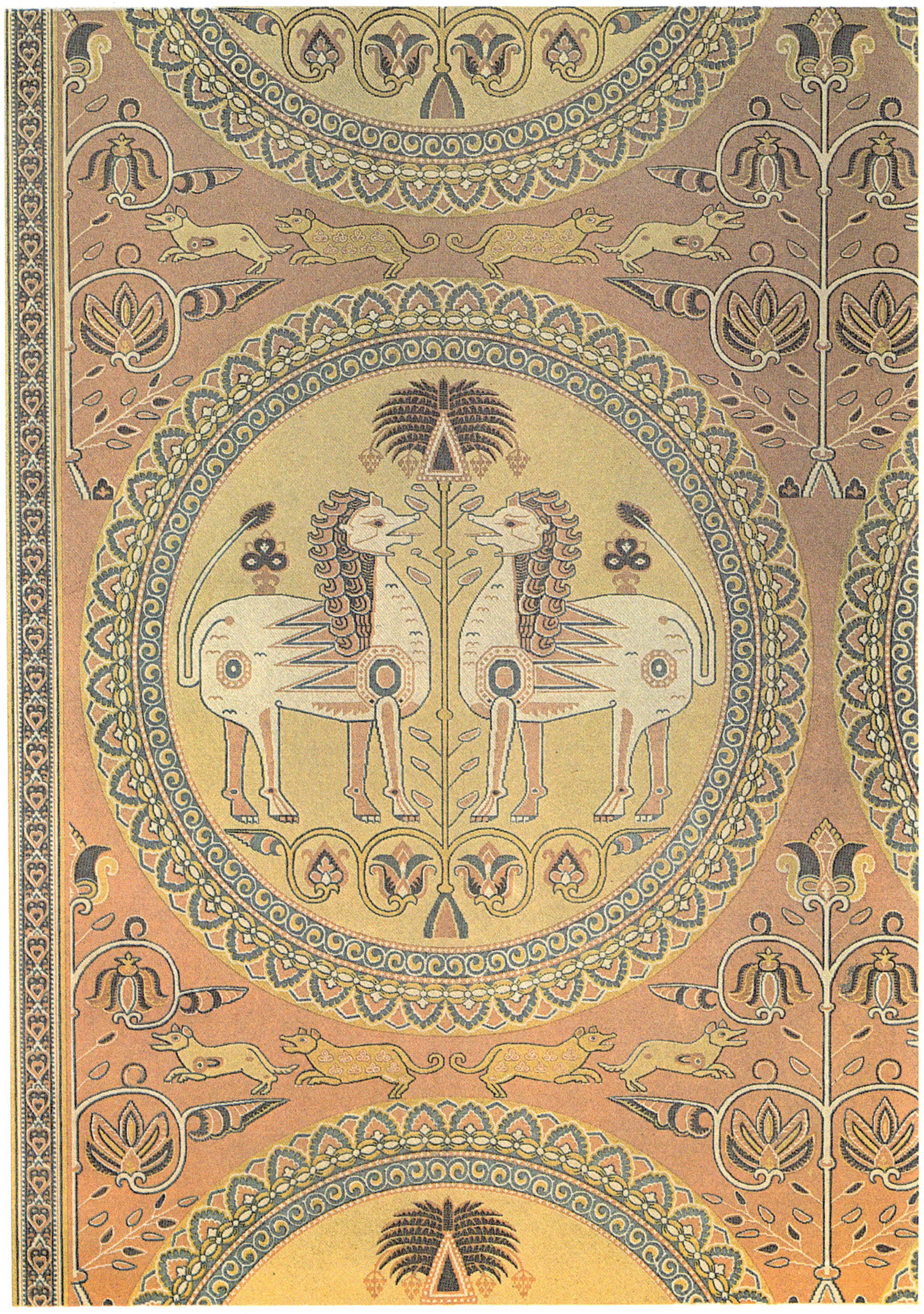

32   Textile wall covering (12th century).

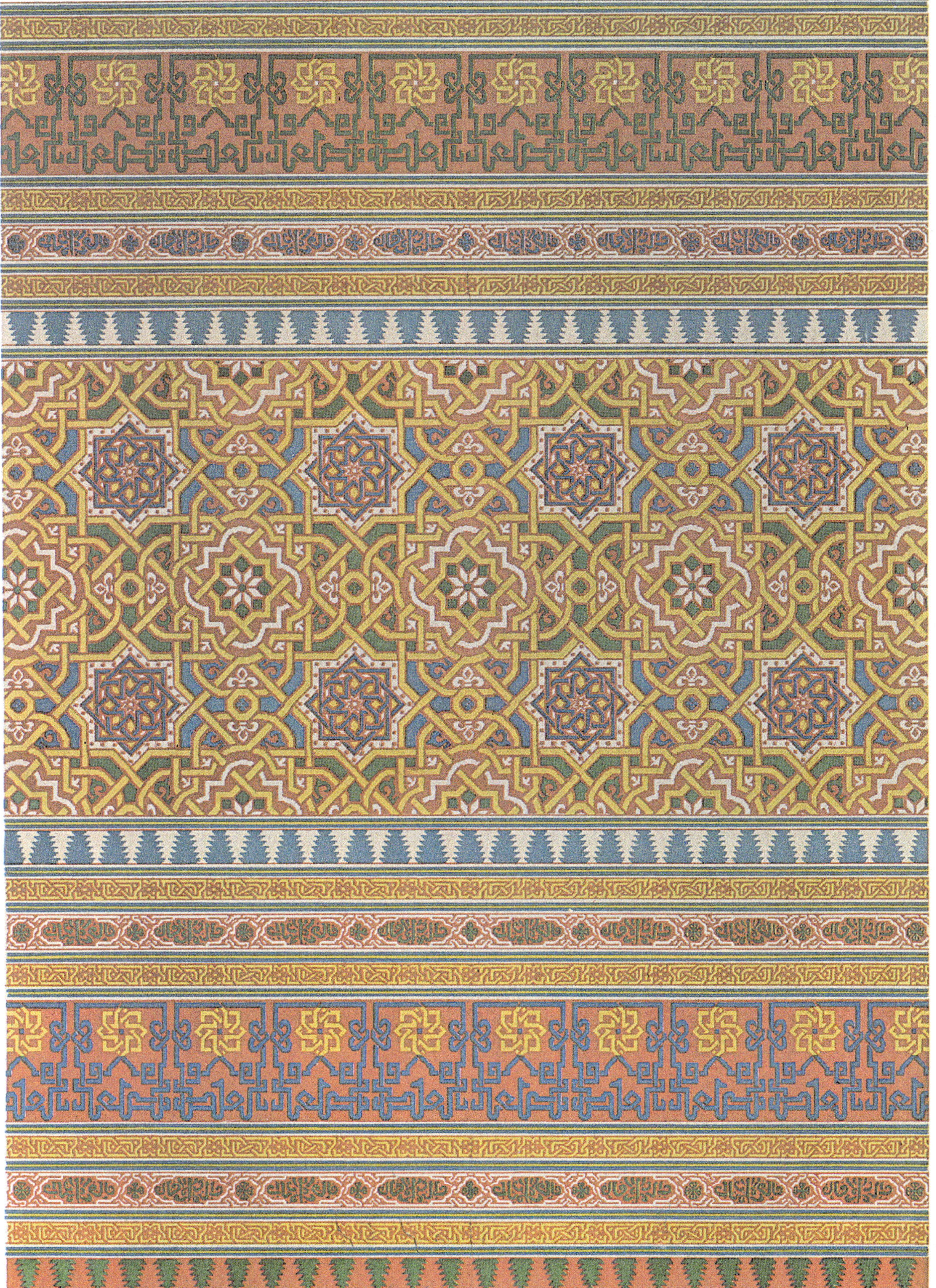

Detail of a textile in a Nivelles (Belgium) collection (14th century).

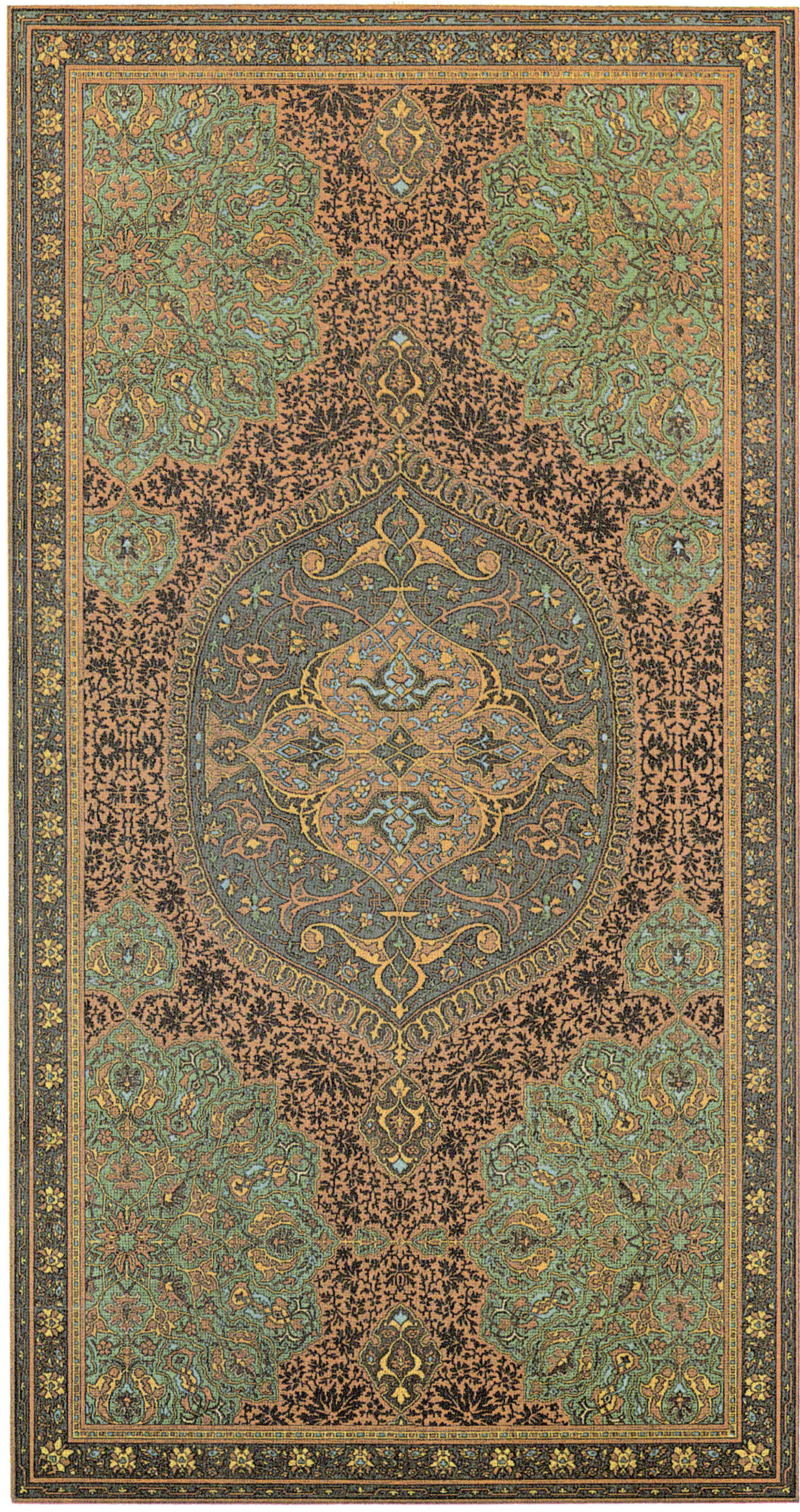

Large velour carpet (18th century).

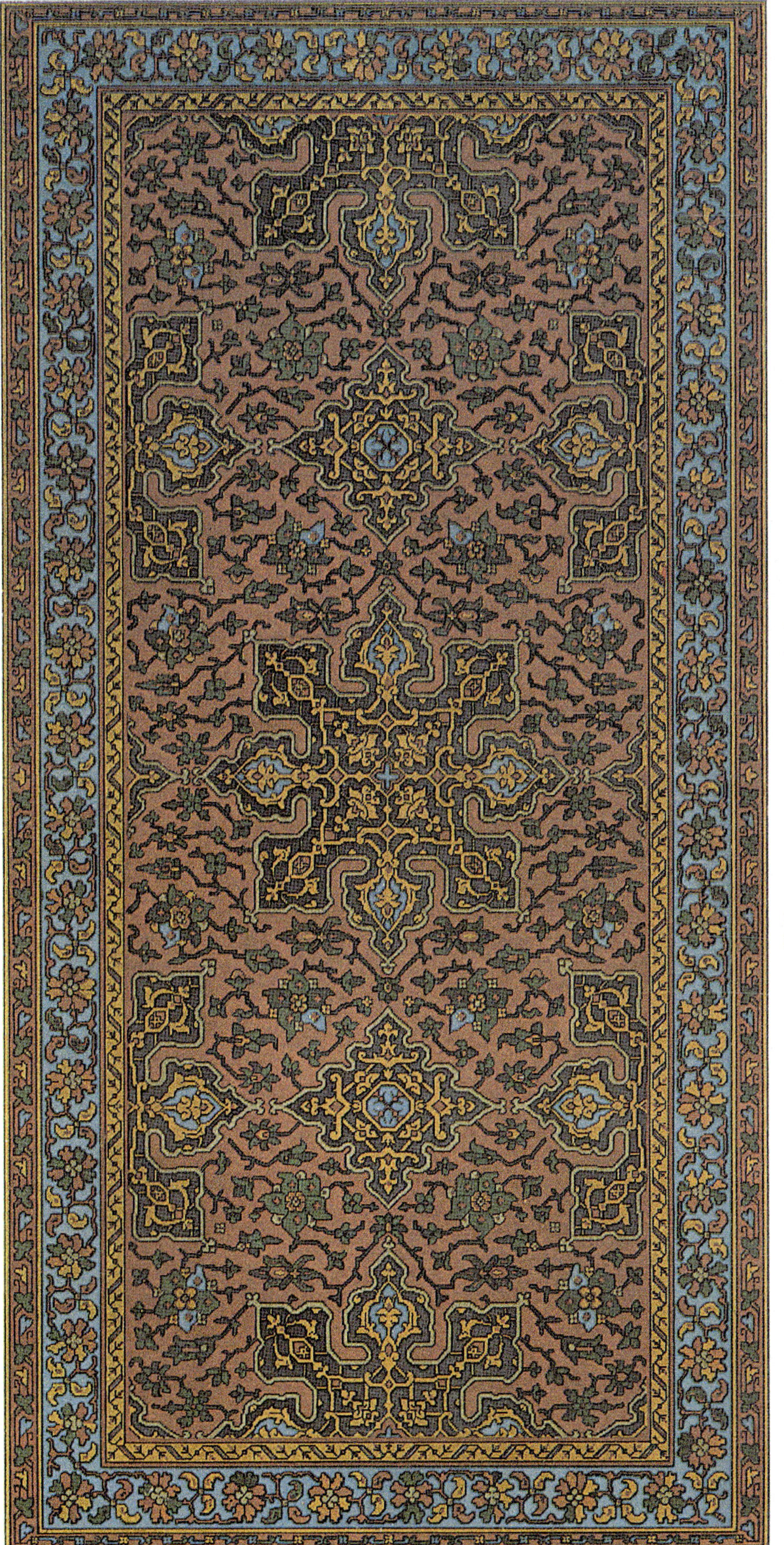

Small velour carpet (14th century).

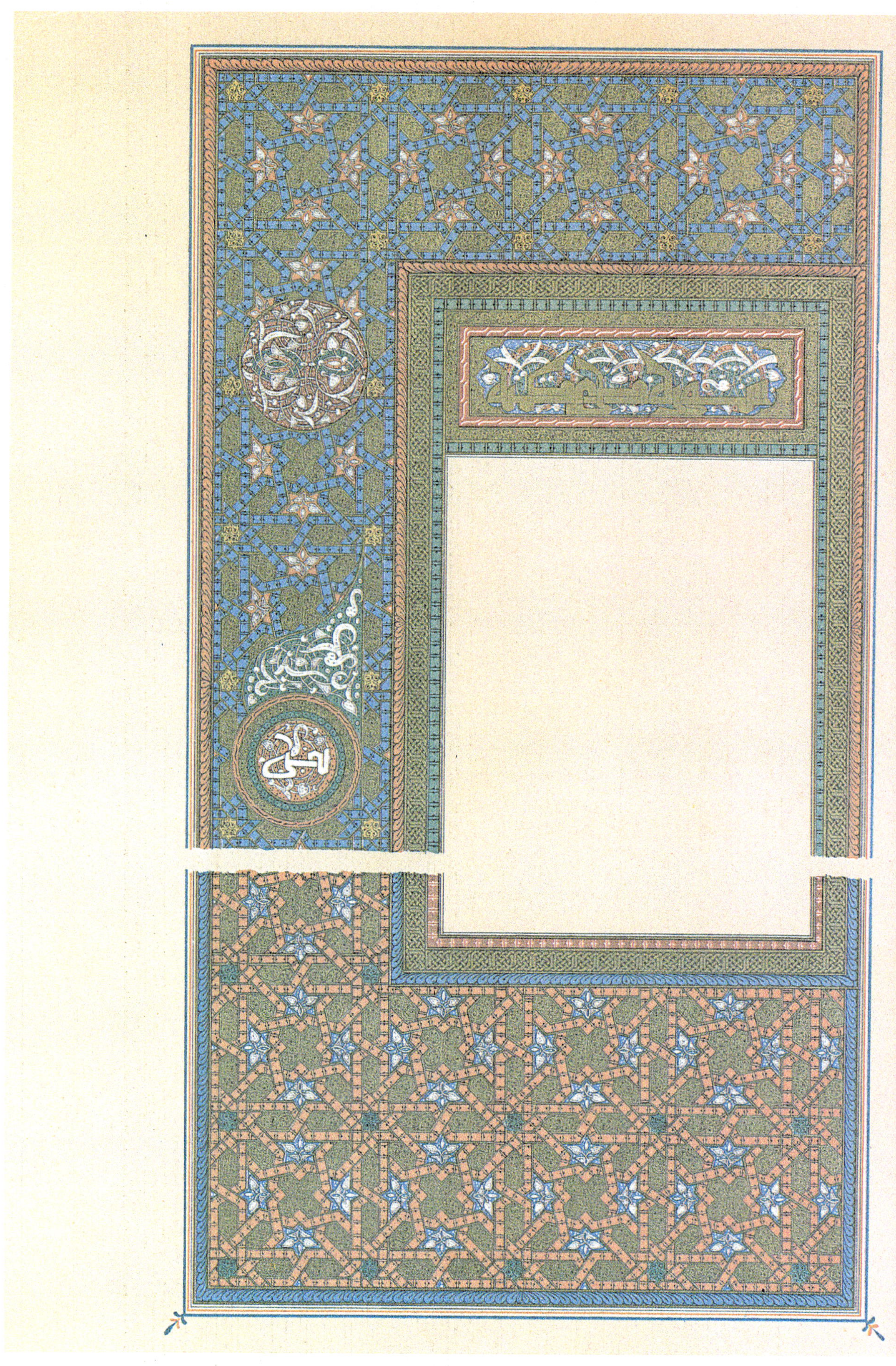

Decoration of facing pages from a Koran made for Sultan Sidi-Mohammed of Morocco in 1768.

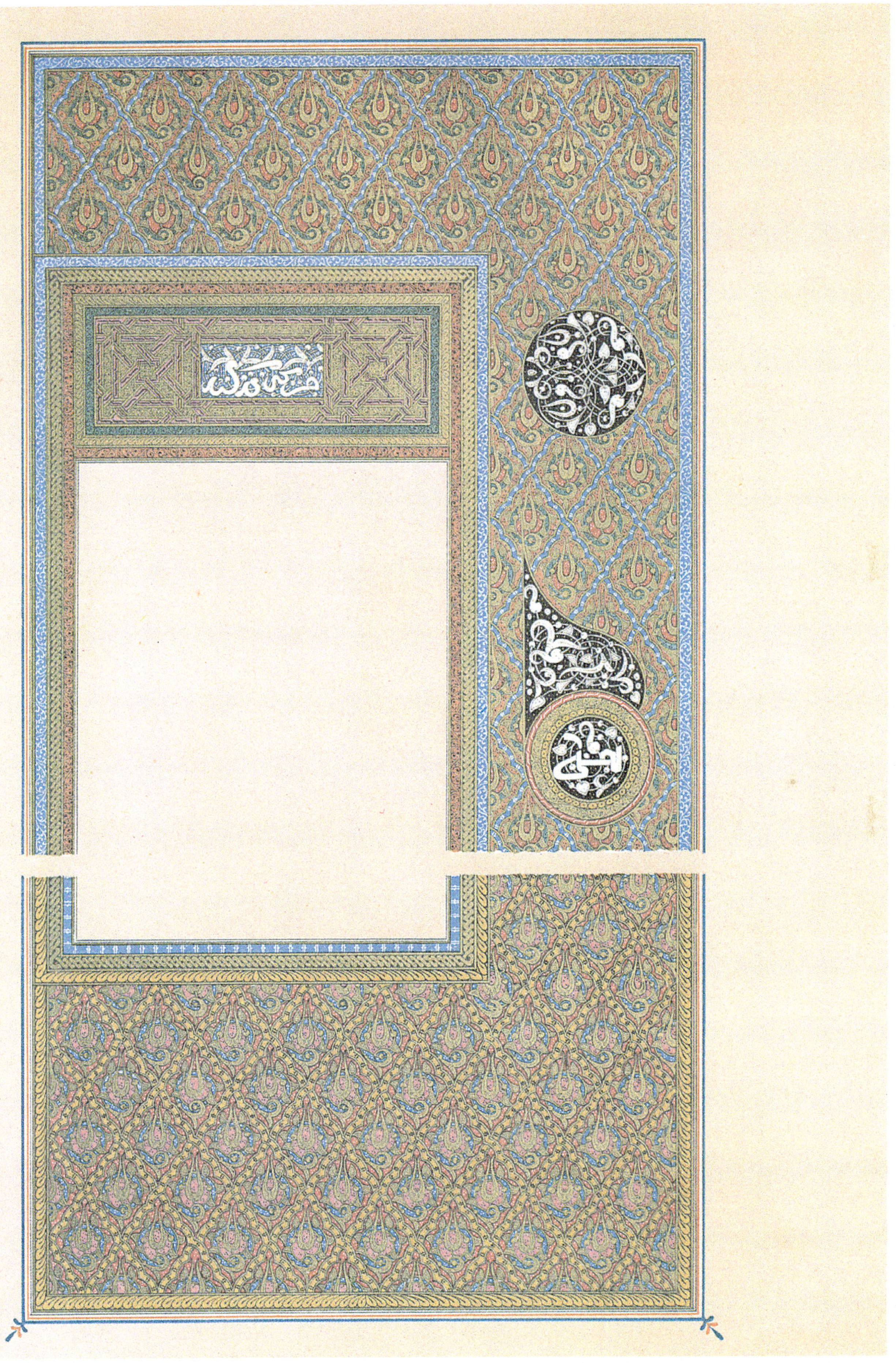

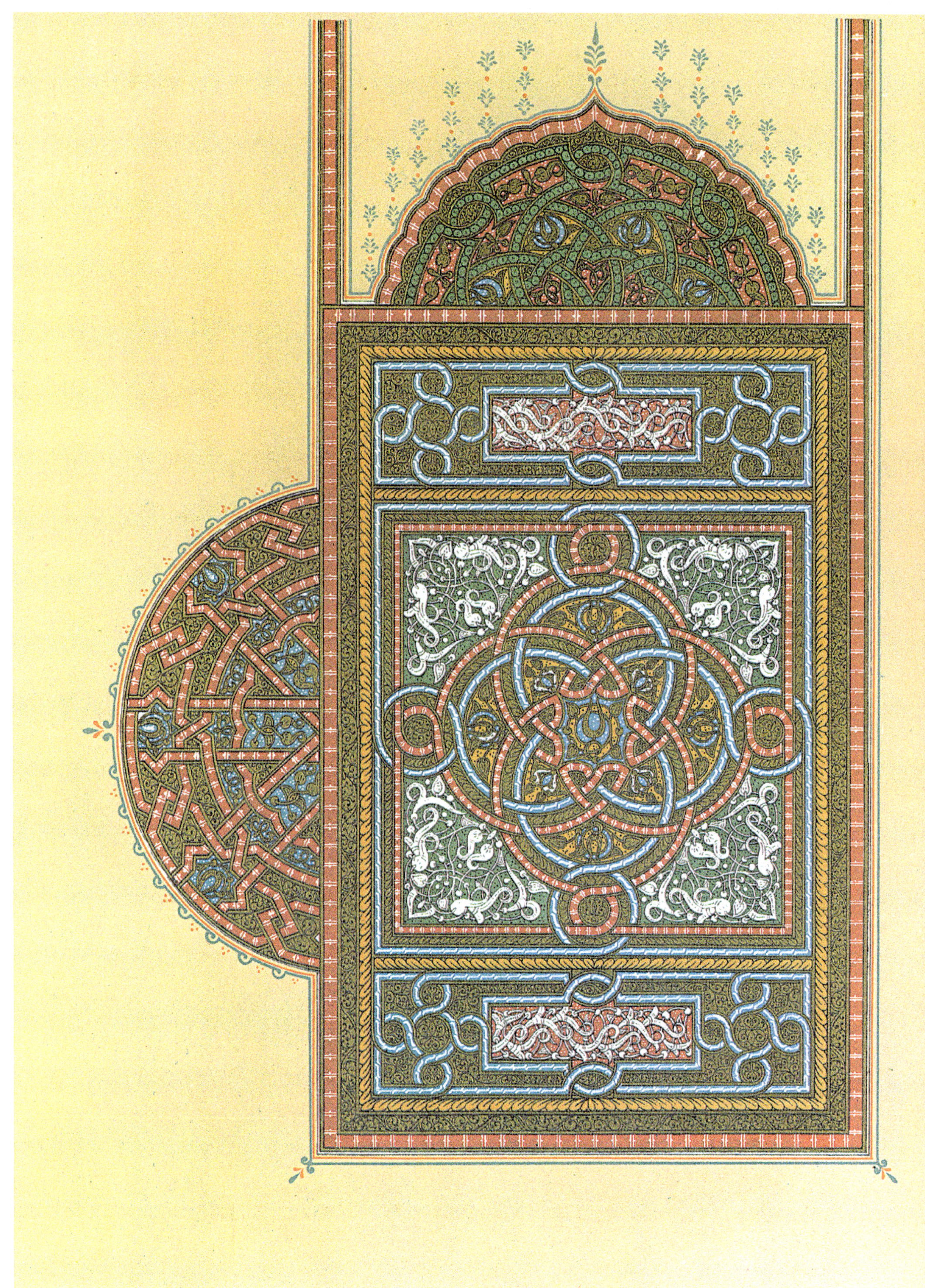

 Facing pages from the Koran of the Sultan of Morocco (1768).

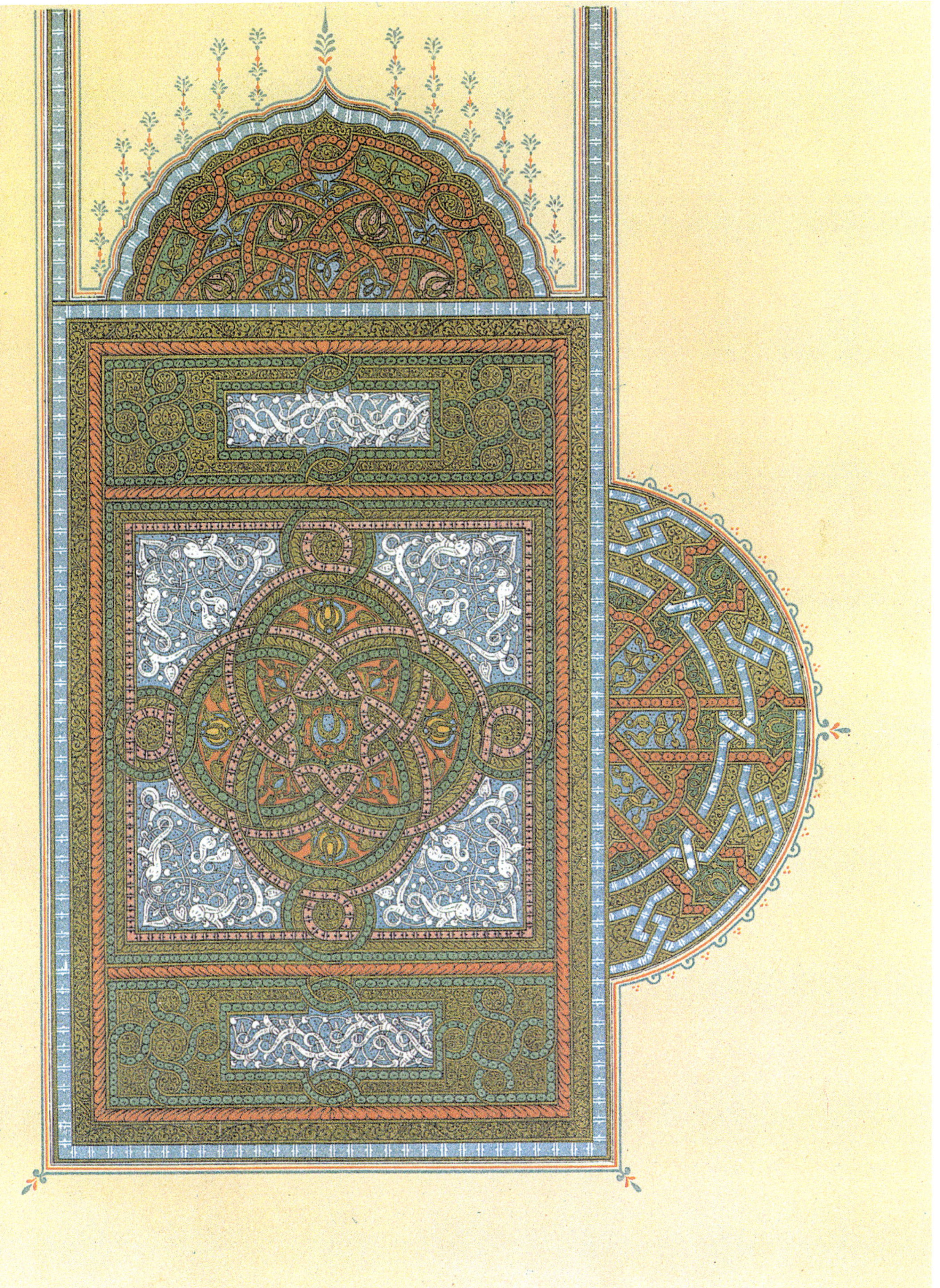

Ornamental details of a Koran from the mosque of Sultan El-Ghoury (16th century).

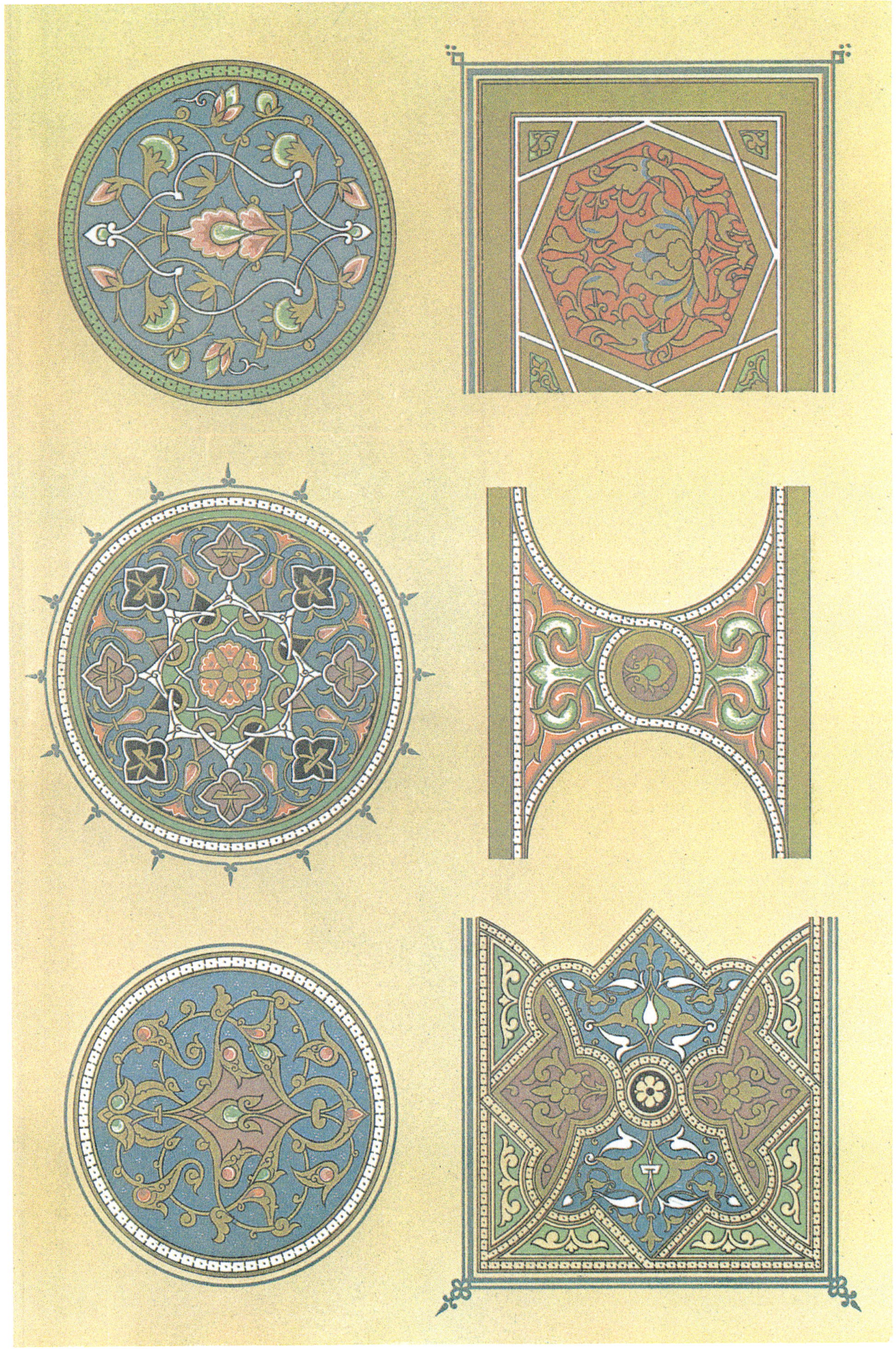

Details of a Koran from the mosque of Sultan El-Ghoury.

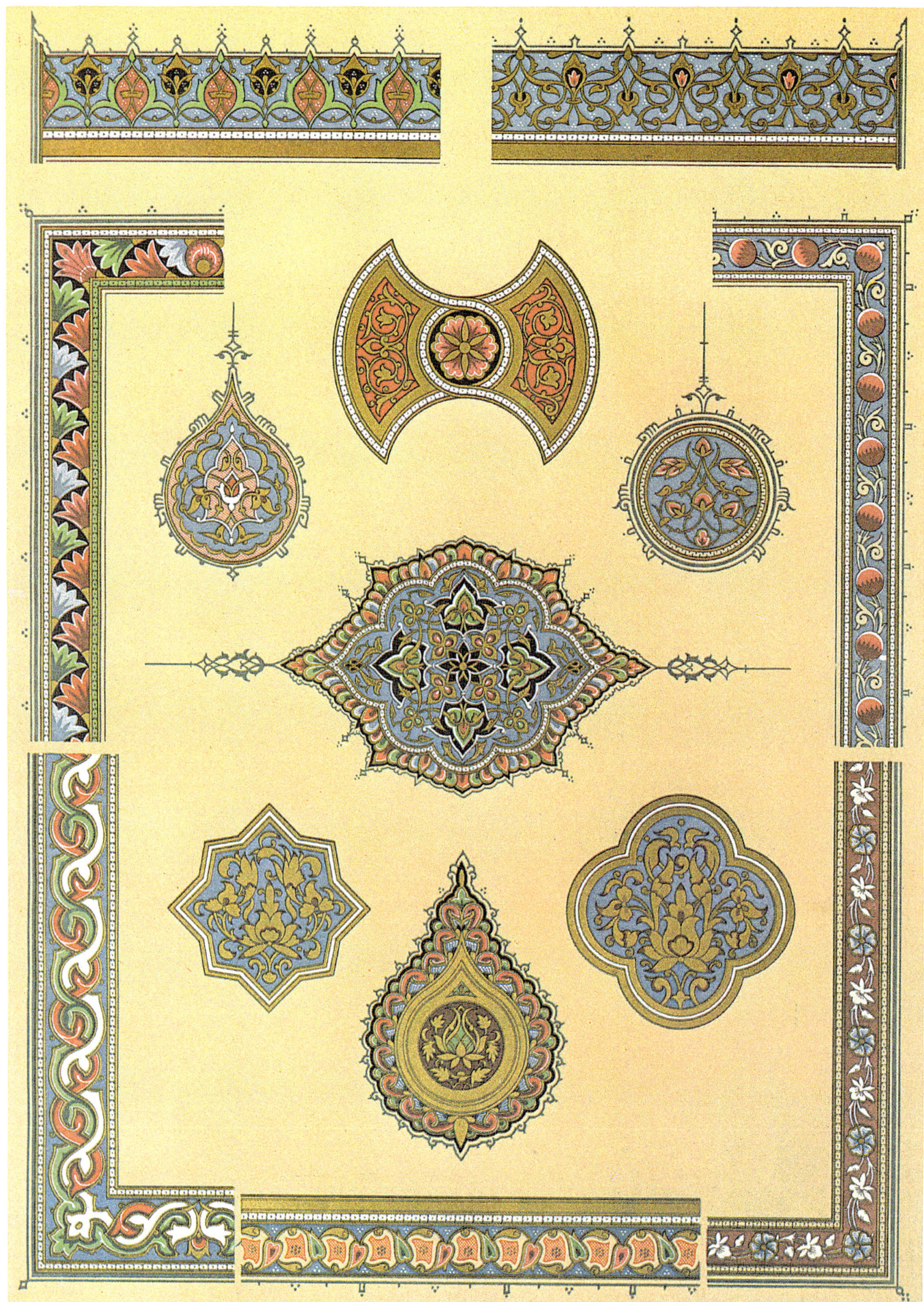

 Details of a Koran from the mosque of Sultan El-Ghoury (16th century).

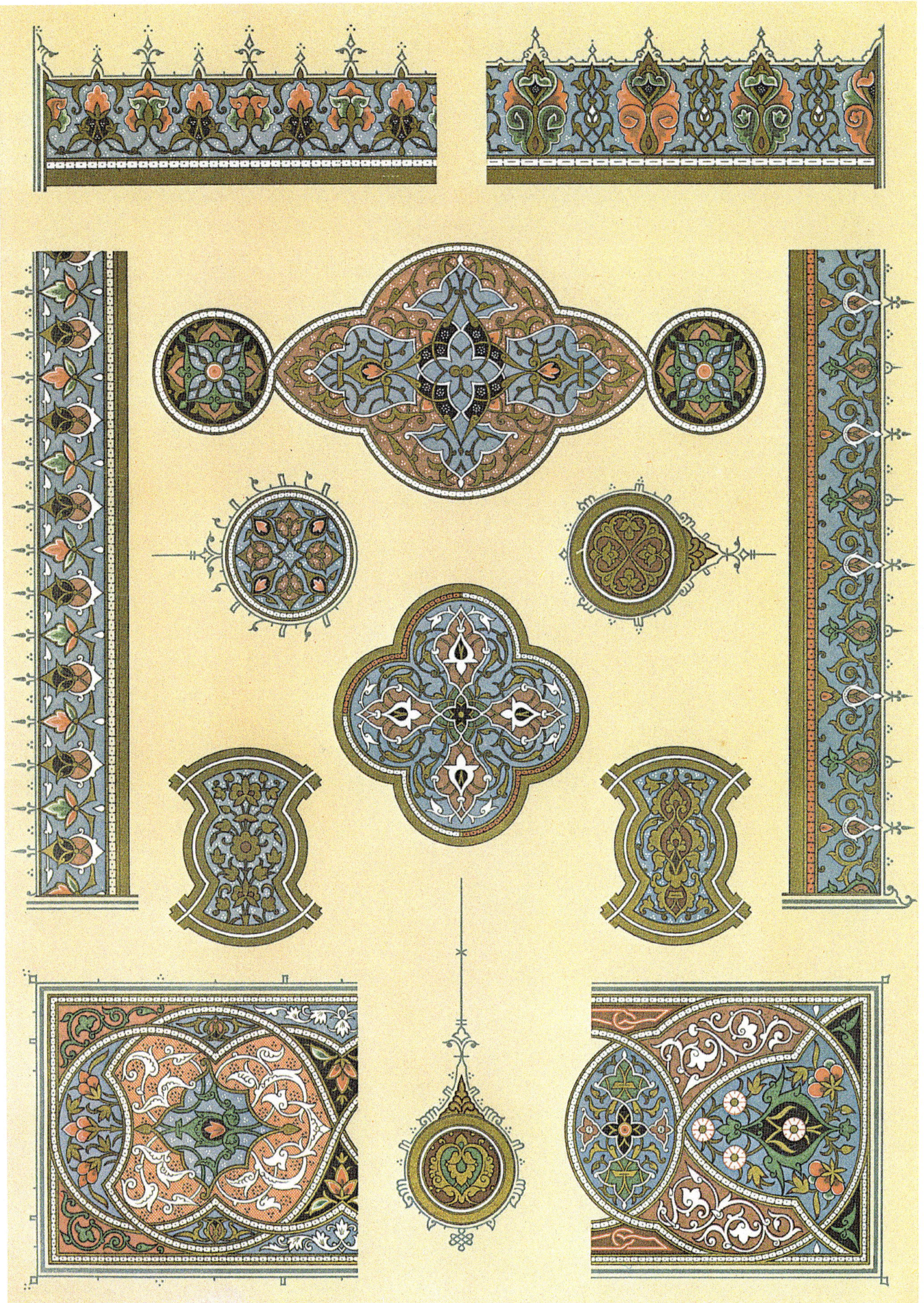

Details of a Koran from the mosque of Sultan El-Ghoury.

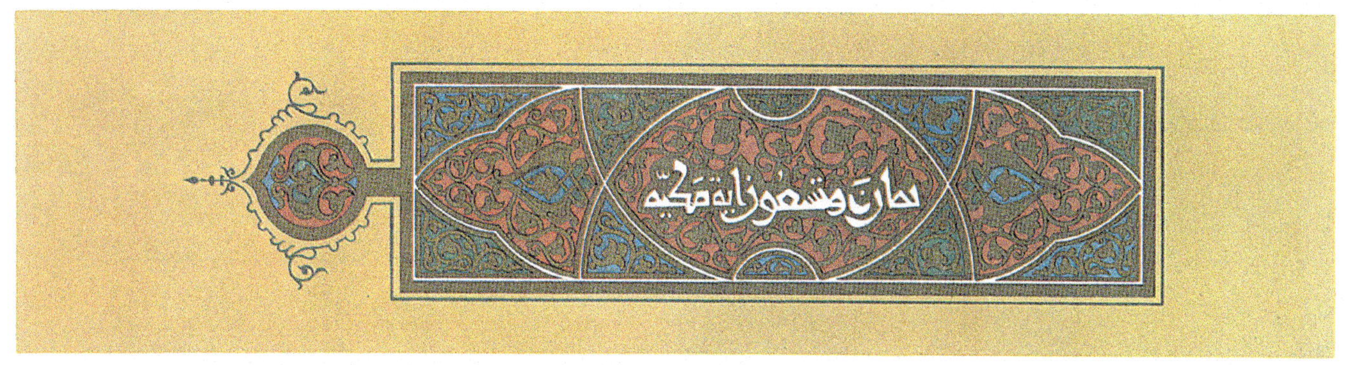

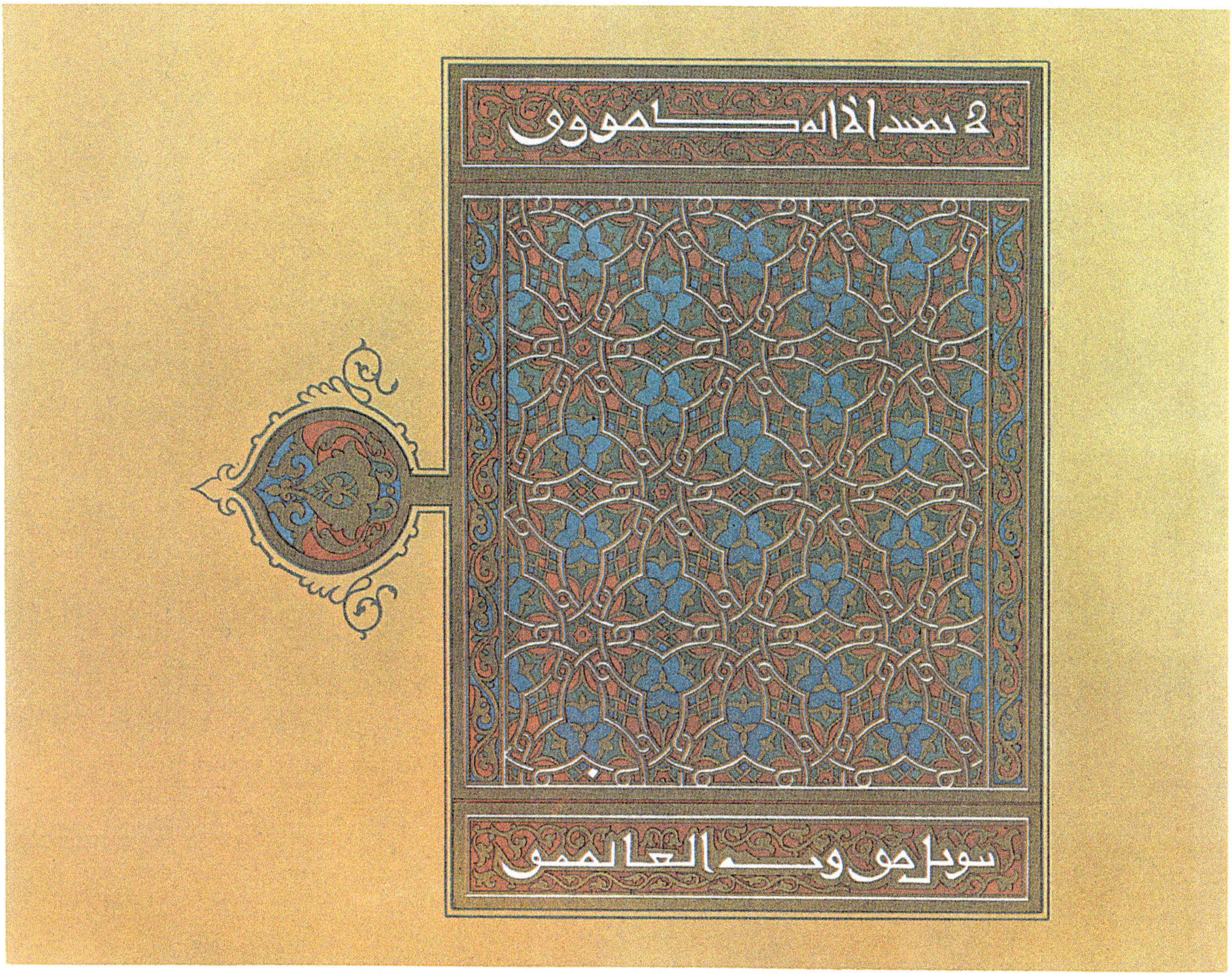

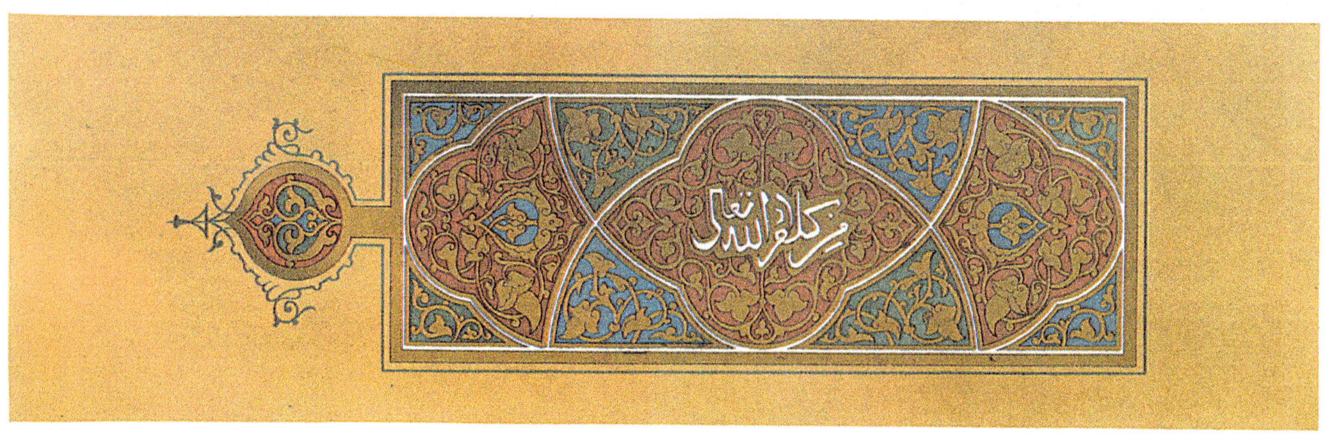

Ornamental details from an Arabic Koran (17th century).

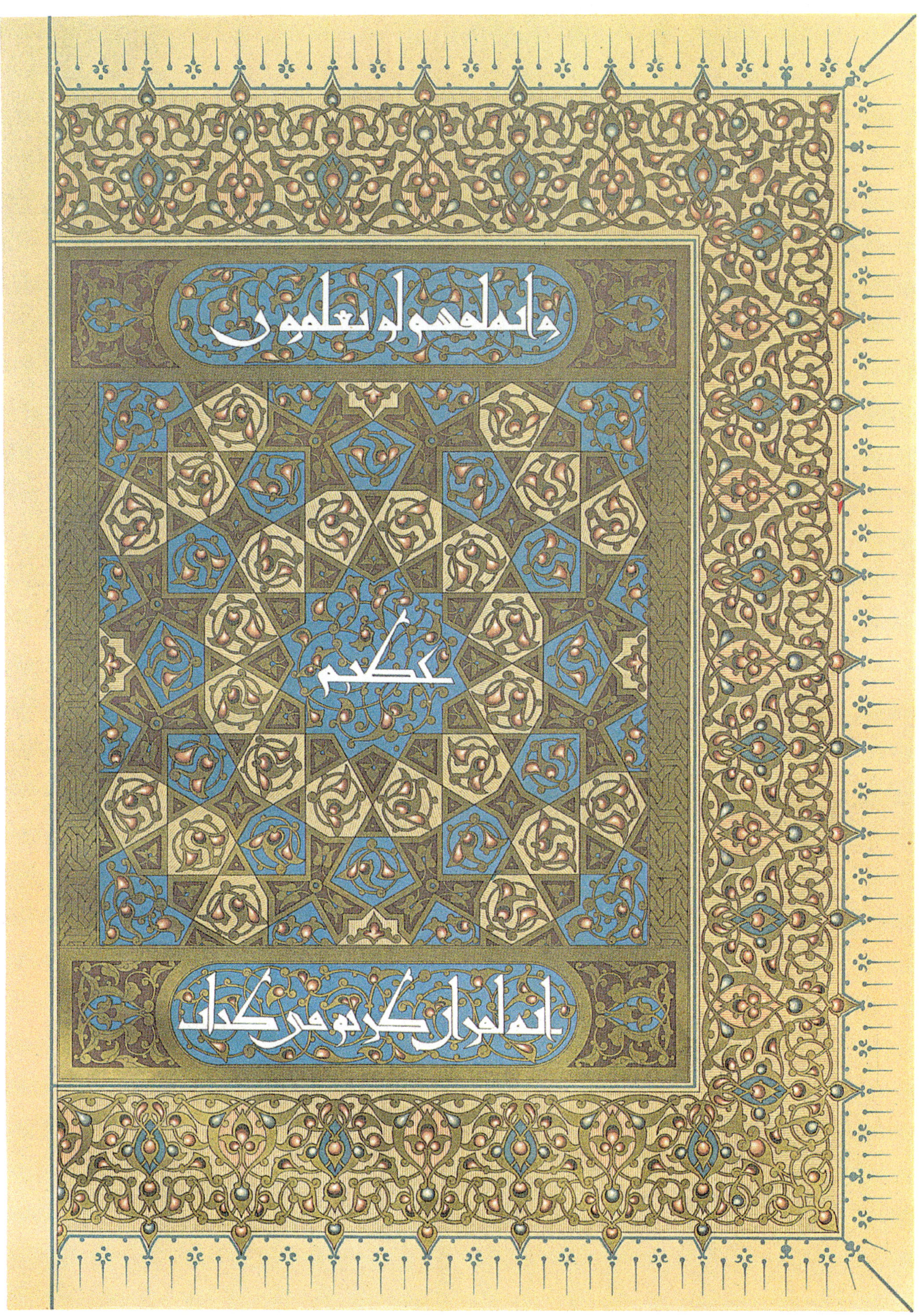

Decorative page of a Koran from the mosque of Qeyçoun (14th century).

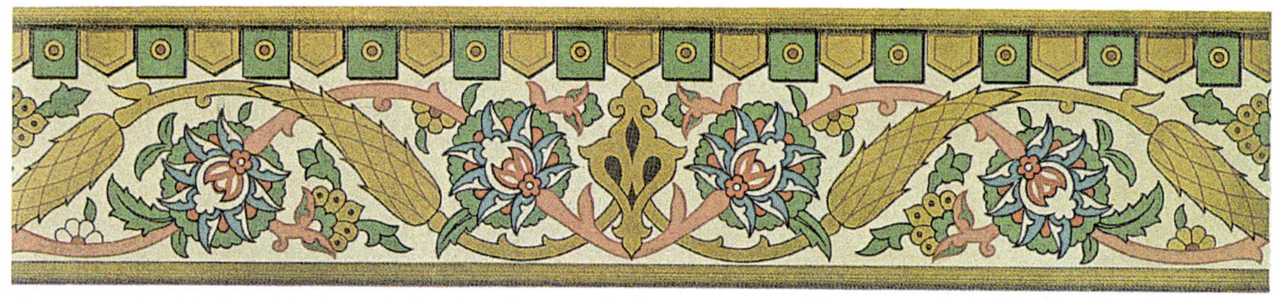

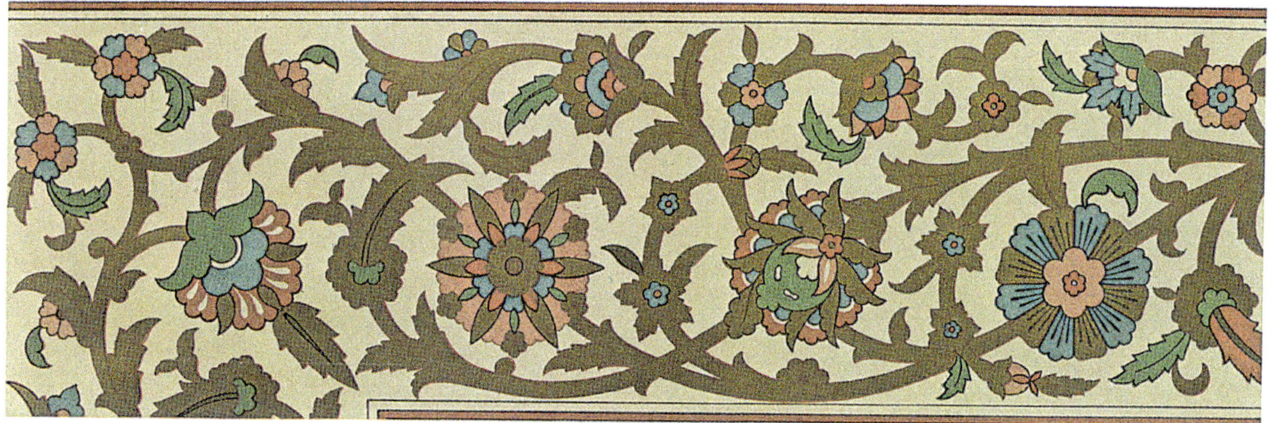

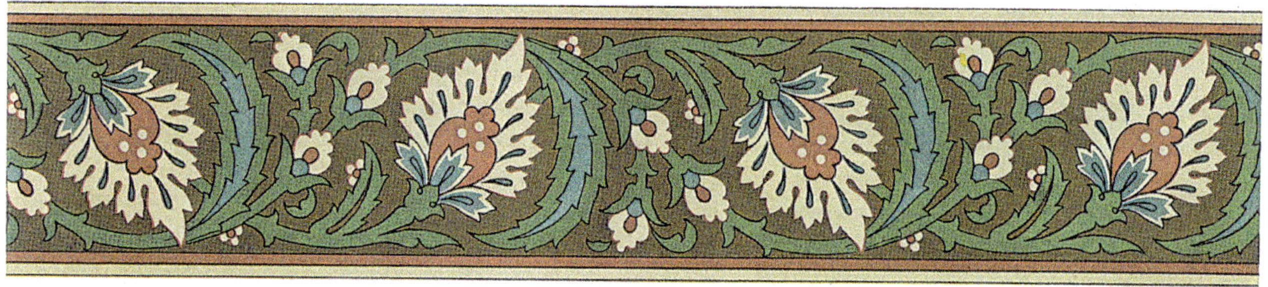

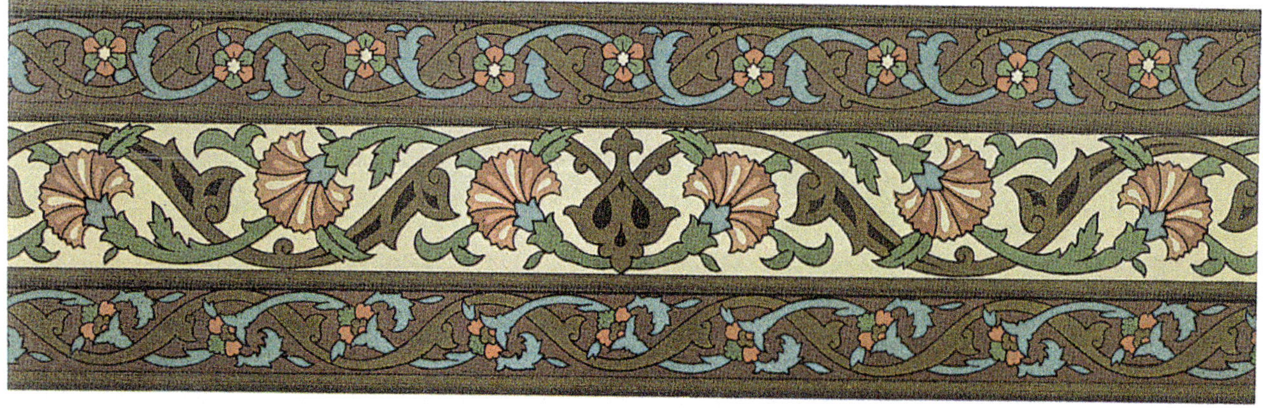

Painted friezes and borders from the smaller rooms in the mosque of Ahmed
el-Bordeyny (17th century).